EDUCATION FINANCE IN THE COMING DECADE

Charles S. Benson

A Publication of the Phi Delta Kappa Educational Foundation

Library of Congress Catalog Number: 75-8377

ISBN Number: 0-87367-406-5

Printed in the United States of America

TABLE OF CONTENTS

Introduction

In preparing a short volume on the topic of financing educational services, I must be selective about the questions and issues discussed. Educational services are provided in formal and in nonformal settings; educational programs are administered by several levels of government; and the administrative officers are subject to control in at least some of their actions by federal agencies and by the courts. Private educational agencies have their own special administrative structures; they are subject to less governmental intervention, but they are not entirely free of it. Schools and colleges are found in densely urban as well as sparsely populated settings; their characteristics reflect their geographic setting. Educational agencies nowadays are beginning to serve very young children. Following long tradition, their chief clients are youth of elementary and secondary school ages, but they serve college and graduate students as well. Finally, in continuing education programs, they offer programs throughout the citizen's life.

Differences in the administrative structure of educational agencies, in their locations, and in the ages and types of students they enroll affect the costs that they sustain, which is to say that such conditions affect the level of financing required. Their efficiency also plays a part in determining their costs.

Education is peculiarly an activity in which the distribution of services to clients of different social circumstances is regarded as important, and recently much effort has gone into trying to rectify conditions that were thought to be inequitable. These efforts have affected the level of financing required, as well as the types of revenue sources employed. The pattern of resource utilization, moreover, is subject to growing control of unionized teachers and faculty.

Education is thus a large, diverse, and complex activity. I do not intend to take up such specialized topics as finance of capital facilities by quasi-public borrowing authorities, improvement of assessment practices, the scope of collective bargaining agreements, or the financing of teachers' retirement schemes. Instead, I intend to concentrate on three issues that are likely to have major impact on the future of public elementary and secondary education.

The first issue is the improvement of family choice in the selection of educational services. The chief economic justification for local control and finance of education is that families can "vote with their feet" and choose to live in the school district that best reflects their educational aspirations. We need to examine how well this process works. We must also recognize that education reformers continue to be interested in establishing arrangements (voucher plans) to allow families to select public or private schools without regard to the existence of local school district lines. This type of arrangement is intended to expand the degree of choice available to families in selecting educational services for their children. The issue here is essentially one of the *structure* of financing of education.

The second issue is whether and how the technological efficiency of schools can be enhanced. Ever since the Coleman Report appeared, critics of education have been able to claim that documentary evidence supports the idea that "dollars do not matter" in establishing the quality of educational programs. On the opposite side, educators have sought to make their objectives clearer and to allocate resources on cost-effectiveness criteria. We need to explore the degree to which educators *can* do these rational kinds of things, in order to assure that their requests for financial resources are favorably regarded by the taxpayers and are adequate to the goals they set. This second issue deals with the question of how well we can determine how much money we need to run the public schools.

The third issue is how we distribute educational services to different client groups and how we raise the money to buy those services in the first place. As is widely known, the courts in many states have found much to criticize in past arrangements for educational finance and have pressured state legislatures to modify those arrangements in the direction of greater equity. But the matter is troublesome because equity is not easy to define in practical terms, while vested interests in the old arrangements are strong. In any case, we shall examine in some detail the current state of the education finance reform movement.

Before dealing with the three main issues, I offer a short chapter on "economic aspects of public education." This is intended to provide some common understanding of financial magnitudes, of the available measures of educational outcomes, and of the economist's frame of mind with respect to public support of school services. I close with a short chapter on some problems raised for the education community by our present high rates of inflation.

This book is written for the nonspecialist. Some members of the education community would undoubtedly like to see a discussion of policy issues dealing with finance and the distribution of education resources. Because I have been writing in the field for 20 years, I cannot claim that all the ideas presented are put down here for the first time. Things are explained that I have tried to explain before. In particular, arguments about vouchers were developed in my book, *The Economics of Public Education*, Chapter 10, and in R. L. Johns, *et al.*, eds., *Economic Factors Affecting the Financing of Education*. However, I believe I have been able to add some new points to the general topic of education finance.

In writing this book I have been assisted by my colleagues in the Childhood and Government Project, Boalt Hall School of Law, University of California, and among them especially Gareth Hoachlander and Elliott Medrich. I also owe a large debt to my constant collaborator, Dorothy Merrick Benson.

CHAPTER I

Education in the Economy

Education is big business. In 1972, instructional staff in public schools numbered 2.3 million, and 45.8 million students were enrolled in grades K-12. Recognizing that the population of the country in 1972 was 208.8 million, we find that one of every 4.3 persons had a direct involvement in the instructional processes of public elementary and secondary education.[1]

In 1971, local public schools cost our citizens $203 per capita; the only item of public general expenditure of all levels of government that ranked higher was national defense, $392 per capita. In that same year, total educational expenditures at all levels of schooling represented 7.9 percent of gross national product; a decade earlier, in 1961, the figure had been only 3.4 percent. It is no exaggeration to say that education is our "largest civilian industry."

Educational Expenditures by Function

In 1969-70, current expenditures for full-time public elementary and secondary schools were $34.2 billion. Of this, $23.3 billion (68.1 percent) was spent on instructional services: salaries of teachers and teacher aides, textbooks, instructional supplies, and the like. Operating and maintaining the school plant added another 3.5 billion (10.2 percent) to the current budget. General administration and fixed charges (insurance, contributions to teachers' retirement, etc.) accounted for $4.9 billion, 14.3 percent. Adding up costs of instruction, building operation and maintenance, and administration and fixed costs, we have a total of $31.7 billion. Thus, 92.7 percent of current budget is consumed in instruction and certain necessary supporting activities.

We make this point to show that only a small portion of the current budget—no more than 7.3 percent—is left to take care of the health needs of students, their nutritional requirements (beyond those their families are able to meet), recreational activities, and travel. True, other state and local agencies are concerned with these matters. However, in the United States, we have not yet organized our state-local services to give any public agency broad responsibility for the full development of young people. In Western Europe, programs for youth tend to be more closely coordinated.

Difference in Expenditures by States and Localities

Another peculiarity of our American educational system is that we tolerate rather wide disparities in educational expenditures. Average current expenditures per student in New York in 1972-73 were $1,584; in Arkansas, they amounted to only $651. Differences in average expenditures are notable as among the states, but they are also quite visible *within* states. New York, long regarded as a leader in educational policy, displayed the following pattern in 1969-70: 15,115 classrooms had expenditures per classroom of less than $12,000, while 37,442 classrooms had expenditures in excess of $24,000.

Revenue Sources for Public Schools

Where does the money come from? In 1973-74, for elementary and secondary schools, 8.2 percent was obtained from the federal government, 40.8 percent from the states, 50.8 percent from local districts, and 0.2 percent from other public sources. These relative shares vary considerably from state to state, however. In Hawaii, 11.0 percent of revenue receipts of the schools in 1969-70 was federal, 85.8 percent was provided by the state government, and only 3.2 percent was local. In contrast, local districts in New Hampshire provided 81.0 percent of revenue receipts and the federal government 7.0 percent, thus leaving only 12.0 percent to be paid by state government.

Extension of Educational Opportunities

In spite of the fact that expenditures and revenue sources vary widely among the states, we have achieved in America a remarkable extension of educational opportunities. In 1940, 44.1 percent of persons in our country aged 20 to 24 had at least four years of high school; in 1972, the figure was 82.7 percent. Taking a longer span of time and a more specific age, 16.8 percent of 17-year-olds had graduated from high school in 1920; in 1971-72, 75.9 percent of 17-year-olds had obtained their diplomas. (Of course, some students receive diplomas at ages past 17.)

At the other end of the public school ladder, it is worth noting that the number of 3- and 4-year-olds enrolled in pre-kindergarten education increased from 439,000 in 1964 to 1,213,000 in 1972. The percent of the age groups represented rose from 5.2 percent in the earlier year to 17.9 percent in the later.

Changes in Educational Costs Over Time

Table I shows that total current spending on public schools in current dollars rose from $15.8 billion in 1963 to $43.5 billion in 1973, a rise of 175.3 percent. In constant dollars, i.e., dollars adjusted to recognize changes in the price level, the increase was more modest: $13.6 billion in 1963 and $22.3 billion in 1973, a percentage gain for the decade of 64.0 percent.

Dollars per student also showed impressive gains. Starting at a current dollar level of $439 in 1963, the expenditures per student crossed the $1,000 barrier 10 years later, for the first time. The percentage rise was 133.7 percent. In real dollars, the percentage gain was 39.5 percent.

What this means is that the broadening of educational opportunities has been accompanied by an increase in the real educational resources laid out per student by the public authorities. This is a major accomplishment for any nation! In our case, the task has been carried forward mainly by local and state governments, units of government that cannot readily avail themselves of these highly productive tax instruments and borrowing powers possessed by central governments.

TABLE I
CURRENT EXPENDITURES IN PUBLIC SCHOOL SYSTEMS, CURRENT AND CONSTANT (1958) DOLLARS, 1963-73

Year	Total Current Expenditures		Current Expenditures Per Student	
	Current Dollars (billions)	Constant (1958) Dollars (billions)	Current Dollars	Constant (1958) Dollars
1963	$15.8	$13.6	$ 439	$377
1964	17.2	14.4	460	385
1965	18.6	15.1	484	392
1966	21.1	16.3	537	415
1967	22.6	16.5	569	415
1968	26.9	18.6	658	454
1969	28.6	18.6	696	453
1970	34.2	20.7	816	495
1971	36.5	20.8	860	489
1972	40.1	21.8	934	508
1973	43.5	22.3	1,026	526

SOURCES: Data on educational expenditures from M. M. Frankel and J. F. Beamer, *Projections of Educational Statistics to 1982-83* (Washington: Government Printing Office, 1974), p. 94; implicit price deflators for state and local government purchases of goods and services from Council of Economic Advisers, *Annual Report, 1970* (Washington: Government Printing Office, 1970), p. 181; and U.S. Department of Commerce, *Survey of Current Business*, Vol. 54, No. 7, July, 1974, p. 10.

Education As Investment

Economists tend to support public outlays on education primarily because they now believe that educational services represent investments in human capital that yield social benefits. Both the notion of "investment in human capital" and the existence of "social benefits" require elaboration.

The investment idea may be explained as follows: National product rises when the output of economic goods and services per member of the labor force goes up. (Of course, it may also rise when the size of the labor force employed increases, but if output per worker is falling at the same time, the situation, not unknown in some parts of the developing world, would hardly be regarded as one that represents a gain in human welfare.) Output per worker may rise as a result of workers' having more or better physical capital goods to use in their jobs, and many economic resources are deployed to supply the work force with improved tools, machines, and equipment in general. Using some of today's output to make more and better capital goods allows us to have more consumer goods tomorrow; this is the general notion of investment.

But under current economic thinking, output per worker may also increase when and as the worker is provided with a higher order of skills in his trade. Indeed, investment in new physical capital may require the worker to have a higher order of training, in order for him to operate the new machinery. In other words, investment in physical capital and the acquisition of new or more highly developed skills in the work force may be complementary, efficiency-enhancing activities.

How are workers' skills improved? According to present-day conventional economic wisdom, they are improved primarily by his participation in processes of schooling and training. We can now see the chain of reasoning: Outlays on education enhance the capacity of members of the work force to acquire the skills they will use in their work; the higher skills allow workers to be more productive, i.e., to turn out a larger supply of goods and services; as an expression of return to this investment process, national output, which is the sum of what workers produce, rises.

If education is a real form of investment, it should follow in our competitive, capitalistic economy that persons who have more education receive higher wages than those who have less. The facts are in accord. In 1970, median annual income of heads of families who were in the 25-34 age bracket and who had completed high school but had not attended college was $10,478. Heads of families in the same age bracket who had four years of college education had a median annual income of $13,538; for those who had five or more years of education after high school graduation, the figure was $15,211. For heads of families in the 45-54 year age bracket, the absolute differences by education level are even greater. For high school graduates, median income was $13,363; for college graduates, $19,179; for those with five or more years of college, $22,534. The association of level of education and income is clear. Indeed, it is possible to translate education-related earnings differentials into rate of return to costs of acquiring different amounts of schooling, and the real rates of return on education are approximately equal to the returns on physical capital investment—10 to 13 percent annually on initial costs.[2]

Before we proceed further, we should digress to acknowledge that not all economists accept the human capital view of the worth of investment in education. Under one dissenting view, the formal educational requirements of most jobs are largely indistinguishable. That is, in a given factory, the middle management positions are likely to be held by college graduates. High school graduates, given a standard amount of on-the-job training, might perform just as well in these positions as college graduates.[3] Educational differences, then, reflect not productivity on the job, but economic power. Once college graduates sit in the management seats, they tend to select other college graduates to sit beside them and, on the other hand, to use the lack of education of workers on the plant floor to defend paying them lower wages. Under this point of view, an education system might be said to exist in order to convince all of us that what we get in the way of life's rewards is what we deserve. Another critical view of the "human capital approach" questions the propriety of having an educational system propelled by maintenance of materialistic values and, in particular, consumerism. More important might be inculcation of values to protect the environment, live in harmony with our neighbors, etc.[4]

So far, the human capital approach holds the field in economics. It has not here been made clear, however, why education should be subject to public support. If the returns to education in the form of higher wages, more interesting work, greater job security, and the like are so apparent, why should not individuals be ready and willing to pay for their schooling themselves, and, if need be, borrow against future earnings to meet necessary costs? In short, if education is so important to individuals, why must the taxpayers carry the financial load?

Actually, this question has two main answers. The first stresses the "social benefits" that educational programs yield. Social benefits are good things from the enjoyment of which it is impossible to exclude anyone. Cleaning up the air in Los Angeles is an example. If a purification scheme were available to rid the smog-afflicted residents of the county from the blight of dirty air, all residents of the Los Angeles basin would benefit in approximately equal measure whether or not they had contributed to meeting the necessary costs of the air clean-up. Suppose the sponsors of the clean air scheme went from household to household asking for financial contributions. Each alert householder could make two easy assumptions: (1) The size of his own personal contribution would be too small to affect the success of the project; (2) if the project was successful, he would receive equal benefits as his neighbor who might, for altruistic reasons, contribute. All economic men would refuse to contribute voluntarily on rational grounds. This is why services providing social benefits ordinarily must be financed under compulsory arrangements, such as taxation.

If it can be shown that education yields social benefits, then a case is established *a priori* for tax support. Some would claim simply that the contribution of education to a rising gross national product is a social benefit, for a high GNP means we are more easily able to support needed social programs, to play a key role in the world economy, etc.

That is, in order to do these things, we are required to sacrifice less than poorer countries; we can give up trivia, not life-sustaining items of consumption. A more reasonable case is to stress that education provides social benefits in the form of better citizenship, a more cultivated society, and lower costs of control of antisocial behavior. There is evidence available on these points. On citizenship, figures show that 73.8 percent of white persons with five years or more of college voted in 1970, while only 47.9 percent of high school dropouts voted. In 1960-61, persons with more than 16 years of schooling spent $97, on the average, for reading material while persons with 9-12 years of schooling spent $46. In 1960, 8.4 percent of the population had four years or more of college and accounted for 1.1 percent of the prison population; persons with five to eight years of schooling accounted for 28.0 percent of the U.S. population and for 40.3 percent of prison inmates. These are clues to the types of "pure" social benefits that education provides.

The second basis for tax support of educational services is easier to explain. If everyone had to pay entirely for his own education or for that of his children, poor families would buy less education for their children than the children's talents would call for. This would seriously impede social mobility, and social mobility remains one of the central tenets of our society.

Education as Consumption: First View
The economist recognizes that education provides individuals with the means to pursue their avocational interests. The more highly educated the person, the more likely he is to spend time and money on reading; writing for plea-

sure; studying in fields outside his work; performing music; attending concerts, lectures, and plays; drawing and painting; and so on. The bases for pursuing such interests are often established in the process of formal education.[5]

It is a somewhat unfortunate phenomenon, possibly, that an individual who receives high-priced education of an investment type is likely at the same time to obtain an unusually large measure of access to cultural education, i.e., education to satisfy consumption demands as defined above. At the same time, an individual who participates relatively little in the formal system in order to improve his vocational standing gains relatively little access to cultural education. To take two extreme examples, consider a young man who attends a private secondary school, such as Exeter, then Harvard College, and Yale Law. He has acquired vocational skills of very great value. At the same time, he has been exposed to the best of Western literature, art, music, and archeology, and, if he wishes to do so, he can easily fit more exotic subjects into his academic program.

On the other hand, consider a youth who attends a public high school of no academic pretensions and then goes to a community college to study computer programming. He, too, acquires a vocational skill of some value, but his opportunities to develop his cultural interests can only be described as relatively meager.

This kind of differential distribution of consumption education is deeply ingrained in our educational system, but it is not an inevitable part of it. It is perverse, in the sense that the Yale law graduate is likely to have more interesting work to do over his lifetime, to feel more in control of his work, and to have a higher level of self-esteem than the computer programmer; he is also likely to have less "free time" to enjoy whatever cultural education he has actually gained. In compensation for our society's demands that many people spend their working hours in performing routinized duties, it would be nice if the society were especially generous to those people in helping them to develop avocational interests. Yet, generosity seems more likely to be displayed toward the future managers and arbiters of our industrial order.

We know that Exeter, Harvard College, and Yale Law admit and offer financial support to a certain number of students of low-income households. Ordinarily, such students must display unusually high academic aptitude. Indeed, one of the functions of any educational system in the modern world is to discover academic talent in young people of all social classes. We defend academic selectivity in admissions to highly valued vocational programs, such as law and medicine, on grounds of our national and personal survival. We want people who have a natural aptitude for law to go to top-rank law schools so that they become prepared to safeguard the institutions that promote justice. We want medical schools to select students who will be good doctors to protect our health. But such reasoning does not establish a case for academic screening to control access to instruction in avocational interests.

Education as Consumption: Second View

So far, all the discussion has been concentrated on the role of education in developing *future beings,* i.e., adults. The child is seen not as a present but as a future person. For example, expenditures on school breakfasts are justified on the grounds that they help poor, hungry children study harder and learn to read and do numbers, all in order to prepare them to enter the work force and secure stable employment. Music specialists employed by the schools are justified on the grounds that they may help a certain number of children develop a lifelong interest in music and, at the same time, possibly discover a future Heifetz.

The idea that children, as a class of present sentient beings, capable of pleasure in today's activities and seeking that pleasure for its sake alone, are deserving of public contributions to increase their present enjoyments does not enter into the economists' justifications of educational expenditure levels. Possibly it should, but this would be a matter of saying that we want to redistribute income from

adults to children in the present time period, without regard to the implications of that distribution for the future.
This is quite a different objective than that of investing in
children's future vocational and avocational capabilities.
Only a highly civilized nation could take the former objective seriously.

CHAPTER II

Economic Efficiency in Education and Household Choice

By definition, economic efficiency is achieved as economic agencies—farmers, manufacturers, school districts—produce outputs that are most highly valued by consumers.[1] If automobile manufacturers shift to heavy cars with low gas mileage at a time when growing numbers of consumers want light cars with high gas mileage, their move would represent economic inefficiency. If school districts emphasize life adjustment when growing numbers of patrons prefer emphasis on basic skills, a condition of economic inefficiency could be said to exist.[2]

The private market economy functions—or is intended to function—at a high level of economic efficiency. Consumers are expected to allocate their incomes so that they waste no dollars on an object of lower utility when an object of higher utility is available. Given the objective of profit maximization, the force of competition leads producers constantly to direct productive resources toward objects of high value to consumers. Centralized public agencies cannot function as the market economy does: Since public agencies are often constrained to supply a single level of output (at any given moment, there is one level of defense readiness in the United States), those who hold a given service in passionate regard and those who are largely indifferent toward it are both likely to be disappointed in the quantity supplied.

However, according to the late Charles M. Tiebout, there is a way out.[3] Wherever possible, let public services be provided by local government. The level of economic efficiency in the public sector can then approximate that in the private, since consumers will "vote with their feet" and choose to live in the community that offers the outputs they value most highly. Those who prefer golf courses and don't care much about schools will select an outdoor sports type of town. Those who feel strongly about schools, libraries, and museums will search out a town that offers services of those types.

This is one way to look at the problem of achieving an optimal distribution of public services. We will need to examine it in some detail. To anticipate our conclusion that Tiebout's model, regardless of its place in economic literature, is not an appropriate guide to educational policy, we will also need to consider alternative devices to improve the economic efficiency of education, of which the best known is vouchers.

The Tiebout Model

Tiebout's 1956 article has become a classic of economic literature. It establishes the chief economic case for localism in government. It is the economic defense of the practice of relying on local taxes to pay for a substantial share of education costs. At the same time, Tiebout's thesis is the economic argument *against* the assumption of education costs by the governmental unit that has constitutional responsibility for the service, i.e., the state.[4] The idea is this: Only at the local level can the consumer take initiative in finding that combination of various types of publicly financed services he desires. At higher levels of government, consumer satisfaction is attainable in lesser degree, because no feasible mechanism exists by which people of similar tastes can sort themselves out and share services to meet those tastes. (If a person likes highways and the state in which he lives has a small highway budget, it is not a feasible solution to suggest that he move to another state.) Hence, any shift of public financial responsibility to a higher level of government diminishes the economic efficiency of the service involved and should be avoided whenever possible.

As Tiebout says,

> The consumer-voter may be viewed as picking that community which best satisfies his preference pattern for public goods. This is a major difference between central and local provision of public goods. At the central level the preferences of the consumer-voter are given, and the government tries to adjust to the pattern of these preferences, whereas at the local level various governments have their revenue and expenditure patterns more or less set. Given these revenue and expenditure patterns, the consumer-voter moves to that community whose local government best satisfies his set of preferences. *The greater the number of communities and the greater the variance among them, the closer the consumer will come to fully realizing his preference position.*[5]

To improve the reality of his argument, Tiebout laid out his assumptions in some detail. They are the following:

1. Consumer-voters are fully mobile and will move to that community where their preference patterns, which are set, are best satisfied.
2. Consumer-voters are assumed to have full knowledge of differences among revenue and expenditure patterns and to react to those differences.
3. There are a large number of communities in which consumer-voters may choose to live.
4. Restrictions due to employment opportunities are not considered. It may be assumed that all persons are living on dividend income.

5. The public services supplied exhibit no external economies or diseconomies between communities.
6. For every pattern of community services set by, say, a city manager . . . there is an optimal community size. This optimum is defined in terms of the number of residents for which this bundle of services can be produced at lowest average cost. . . .
7. The last assumption is that communities below the optimum size seek to attract new residents to lower average costs. Those above optimum size do just the opposite. Those at an optimum try to keep their population constant.[6]

Though each of the assumptions is interesting, and though each may attract the fancy of the reader, we discuss two that appear to be crucial in considering the implications of the Tiebout model for educational services. These are numbers 1 and 5.

Household Mobility

Changing residence is not a costless process. Costs are associated with the search for a new dwelling and moving of household goods. For persons who live in owner-occupied dwellings, a number of other costs are associated with transfer of property. In addition, there may be psychological costs: Moving residence is sometimes a traumatic experience, especially for young children. The upshot is that the costs of "voting with one's feet" may well outweigh the anticipated benefits to be derived from public services in the new neighborhood. At best, the Tiebout solution, based as it is on geographic entitlement to public services, is a cumbersome means of matching household preferences to type and quality of services.

Assume that a family's income rises by $4,000 a year over a three-year period. Let the family have two children, and let the adults in the family decide they would like to spend a quarter of the increased income on the education of their school-age children. The costs of moving might easily exceed $1,000, in addition to which there is the disruption of family life that the move entails. If the family is middle-class and lives in a house it owns and which has appreciated in value, the family either will have to pay a substantial capital gains tax or buy a house that costs considerably more than their old house did when they first bought it. Since property tax assessments are commonly revised at the time a parcel of real estate changes hands (but not frequently otherwise), the family may find itself paying higher local taxes.

On the other hand, suppose the family used private schools. It might be paying tuition fees at $1,500 a year per child. Given the increase it has obtained in its income, the family is now prepared to pay $2,000 per child in annual tuition fees. This increase of one-third in financial provision should allow the family to find schools that offer a considerably higher grade of service. Private education, accordingly, allows a family to adjust its preferred expenditure pattern rather precisely to changes in its level of income. The same process could be approximated in the public sector if families were allowed to enroll their children across district lines under the following conditions: (1) that their district of residence would transfer to the receiving district a sum equal to the annual recurring costs that would otherwise have been spent on the students in the home district, and (2) that the parents pay for any positive difference between costs per student in the receiving district and in the home district. This is a simple procedure by which the stultifying restriction of geographic entitlement could be circumvented, in order to allow parents to express their demands for educational services in more convenient and reasonable ways.

In his basic assumption about household mobility, Tiebout postulates that preference patterns are "set." (See Assumption 1, quoted above.) Even if we accept this point, we must recognize that children's preferences for schools are not identical, nor are parents' preferences necessarily identical for all of their children. Parents may prefer the school of District X for their first child and that of District Y for their second. Under Tiebout's model, one or the other of these preferences must be disappointed. More to the point, education is intended, among other things, to change the preferences of those who are involved in it. If a close fit is to be maintained between preferences for services and services actually received, then, given the dynamic action of successful education on the pattern itself, Tiebout's model calls for considerably more moving about of households, and thus considerably higher costs of moving, than one might first envisage.

The Tiebout model does not readily encourage effective expression of choices by students. For example, suppose a certain high school student is dissatisfied with the school he attends, for apparent good reason. He may have a number of siblings, all of whom are reasonably well satisfied with their schools. If the price of putting the high school student into a more intellectually satisfying environment is uprooting the whole household, the price is not likely to be paid. The situation is made more distressing by the fact that, assuming the student is below school-leaving age, legal obstacles are commonly placed in the way of his taking a respite from an unfortunate situation and studying at home for a year. Thus, where geographic entitlement rules, and taking account of the difficulties that attend "voting with one's feet," the courts appear to demand that students sit out unsatisfactory learning conditions.[7]

Another disadvantage of the Tiebout model is that rich households are empowered to obtain a higher level of satisfaction in the public sector than poor households. This is a general consequence of the model's approximation of the market distribution of services. In all known free enterprise markets, those who have greater purchasing power obtain more goods and services than those who have less. Our whole capitalist incentive structure is built on this proposition. Thus, the very strength of Tiebout's model, fitting services to preferences, implies unequal and income-biased distributions of public services, as long as household incomes are unequal.

We need to see how this unequal distribution of services works in education, but, first, let us consider why it might be regarded as unfortunate. The author has recently written,

If educational services, like medical services, were provided mainly in the private sector, no one would be surprised to discover that poor people received a lower quality education than the rich. American schools, on the contrary, are largely to be found in the public sector, and ironically, the *publicly financed and administered* system of education deals shabbily with the poor. *A guiding principle of public operation, however, is equal treatment of equals.* If a set of families enters a state park to go hiking, that group would be shocked indeed to discover that the scenic trails were reserved for its richer members and that only barren and rocky paths were held open for the poor. Nevertheless, our public schools operate in such a discriminatory way. Those who doubt this assertion might advantageously walk through Benjamin Franklin High School in East Harlem and then through South Commack High School in Suffolk County, Long Island. If this is not convenient, any inner-city high school could be compared with any high school in a suburban community where average family income is above $14,000.[8]

Furthermore, education is often viewed as one of our chief instruments to provide social mobility. If educational services are distributed positively with respect to income, then the advantages in entering the job market otherwise held by high- and middle-income youth will be reinforced by the operations of the public sector.

Now, why does the Tiebout model produce such an insidious distribution of services in the specific case of education? Let us recognize that education is ordinarily viewed as an important service by households with school-age youth; those households have a significant and immediate stake in the quality of schooling provided to their children. Next, let us imagine that in earlier times, places such as Beverly Hills, Calif.; Shaker Heights, Ohio; Scarsdale, N.Y.; Greenwich, Conn.; Clayton, Miss.; and Newton, Mass., were known locally to be offering a superior standard of schooling. It is natural to expect that educationally minded families would be attracted in substantial numbers to these places and that they would bid up the value of land on which to build houses. This is only to say that where geographic entitlement rules, superior services will attract trade and that the resulting influx of residents will result in higher land prices. As the price of land went up, it probably would make sense for builders to place large, high-priced houses on the building lots. In any case, houses located in places known for superior services should carry a higher price than identical houses elsewhere: The difference in value is a measure of demand for the given public service or set of services. This is "capitalization" of locational advantage on the side of service provision. The high prices of residences establishes a scheme of rationing under which only high-income households typically gain access to school programs like those offered in Beverly Hills, Shaker Heights, etc.[9]

If the residential properties are of sufficiently high value, or if industrial or commercial properties are attracted to the locality (such properties ordinarily serving to increase the size of local tax base while adding no appreciable cost to school district operation), the school tax rate is likely to creep downward.[10] School tax rates are relatively low in Beverly Hills, Clayton, and Greenwich for just these reasons. Capitalization of land values on the tax rate side may reinforce capitalization on the service benefit side. The privileged suburb would offer the attractions both of superior school services *and* a low school tax rate. Housing values would reflect both types of benefits.[11]

Once these "lighthouse districts" come into existence, the old residents have strong financial incentives to screen new residents carefully. The reason is that just as a favorable local fiscal situation produces capitalized values in residential properties, so the development of unfavorable conditions can destroy those capitalized values. A person who has paid $250,000 for a house and land in a privileged district will not easily accept deterioration in standard of local services or increases in local tax rates if such developments lop $100,000 off the value of his property.

Let us concentrate on the matter of local tax rate and see what is required to keep the rate from rising with an influx of new residents.

To hold the tax rate and individual household tax bills constant, at least three criteria must be met: (1) newcomers must have no more school-age children per family than the average of residents and they must cause no increase in capital outlay; (2) newcomers must purchase houses of value at least equal to the existing town average; and (3) newcomers must possess no general propensity to require special school or nonschool expenditures on their behalf. A community may assure that these three criteria are met by carefully constructing zoning and building regulations. Land may be zoned strictly for single-family houses built on lots of at least one acre. Limits may be placed on the number of bedrooms in new apartments and condominiums. The town may require private construction and maintenance of sidewalks. Many communities prohibit overnight street parking, thereby forcing construction of parking facilities on land that might have been used for housing. . . . All of these requirements increase the cost of housing, which in turn effectively screens lower-income households from middle- and upper-class areas. Since lower-income households tend to have larger families and children needing specialized school services, these practices also tend—directly and indirectly—to satisfy requirements one and three. *In short, the structure of the educational system produces stratification of communities by income level and, to some extent, by family size and certainly by differential education requirements of young children.*[12]

To some extent, the local tax rate problem is ameliorated by changes now occurring because of the education finance reform movement. However, while these changes protect communities against accepting families that have larger than community-average numbers of children and families that occupy low-priced housing, they are not yet very effective in protecting communities from the fiscal consequences of accepting families with children that are unusually costly to educate. Moreover, practically all of the reform proposals so far adopted imply an increased role for state government in setting educational policy. The almost inevitable results are to increase uniformity of standards and to reduce local initiative. These changes fly in the face of the Tiebout model's stress on the existence of numerous communities that display substantial differences in service patterns.

Externalities Among Communities in Production and Consumption of Local Services

Recall Tiebout's assumption that there are "no external economies or diseconomies between communities."[13] The basis for public intervention in the supply of educational services *is* the assumed existence of spill-overs from one community to the next. Further, if a given metropolitan area has many different communities of different size and service standards, how can education services fail to display externalities among communities? To hold otherwise is practically to assert that education benefits and costs are held within the single household.

If families with children who perform well in school are allowed to cluster in socially isolated school districts, the children excluded from such districts are likely to suffer because teachers will not be pressured to offer intellectually stimulating instruction. Thus, clustering of families by tastes offers benefits to some children and injury to others.[14] The effects cannot be confined within single school districts. When potentially high achievers find themselves in a school of generally low academic standards, their potential is more likely to escape notice than if they were in a school of high standards. This means that educational isolation by parental tastes can abort the operation of the talent identification function (the screening function) that educational systems are supposed to perform. When this happens, the whole society loses, not just the single school district. Furthermore, we have seen that one of the social benefits of education is inculcation of democratic values in the rising generation. To find oneself as a student in a poorly supported, socially isolated school setting can hardly be regarded as consistent with the fair treatment democratic societies are supposed to give their members.

Other Problems With the Tiebout Model

We consider two other problems with the Tiebout model as a guide for resource allocation in education. The first has to do with "complementarities" in the provision of public services, and the second with economies of scale.

In Tiebout's analysis, local public services are regarded as having independent effects on households. This is patently not the case with respect to education and a number of related services. It may profit a child little to have the chance to attend a good school if he is poor, has serious health problems, and lives in a community that is substantially indifferent toward provision of public health services.[15] Likewise, school, public library, and recreational services can reasonably be seen to complement each other. From the child's point of view, the standard of any single service is not important. What matters is whether a whole range of interrelated services all are up to an acceptable standard. When this condition prevails, children benefit and education advances, but opportunities for exercise of Tiebout choice diminish. From the point of view of young persons, it would seem especially important to aim for a generalized acceptable standard of local public services, extending across the main activities in which children are involved—education, supplementary education services, libraries, recreational programs, and services that support the family condition such as health, welfare, public transport. The point is reinforced when we consider that the private sector seeks to shape the tastes of the young in order to increase profits, using the means of television, radio, magazines, etc.

The problem of economies of scale has to do with the facts (1) that children learn not just in school but also in their contacts with libraries, zoos, science centers, museums, theaters, orchestras, and so on; and (2) that such rather highly specialized activities are commonly found only in large centers of population. For example, assume one-half of 1 percent of the population is sufficiently interested in science and technology to make frequent use of a facility such as the Science Museum in Cambridge.

If geographic entitlement strictly controls access to such facilities, which is to say that the service is not otherwise subsidized, then a city of 100,000 population, which would have 500 regular users, could by no means justify the multi-million dollar annual budgets of such institutions. A region of 5 million population, however, could. As the number of users increases (up to the point where users are unduly distracted from their enjoyment by having to queue up or, in general, by being crowded), cost per user decreases. Highly specialized services, thus, demand large cities or metropolitan regions to sponsor them, under geographic entitlement. Libraries might appear to be an exception, for even small towns have libraries. (However, that does not establish that small town libraries are of high quality. To the inquiring mind, the best library, generally speaking, is the largest.)

In elementary and secondary education itself, it is generally assumed that economies of scale do not exist, though diseconomies may. As Cohn states, "The best educated guess . . . is that the condition of decreasing returns to scale is the most likely state of the education industry."[16] However, as Cohn notes, empirical studies of the point do not deal adequately with the relationship between size of the producing unit and *quality* of educational program.[17] Some of our most well regarded high schools, such as New Trier, in Illinois, are much larger than the typical U.S. secondary institution. New York City continues to demonstrate the effectiveness of high schools that are not only large but specialized, e.g., the Bronx High School of Science.

Our conclusions on the problem of economy of scale are the following: First, it is probably desirable to have big cities within effective commuting range of concentrations of youth whenever this can be arranged. Accordingly, it would be inappropriate on the grounds of economy of scale to split big cities into small, autonomous units, even though it might be advisable to devolve administrative control of certain family-oriented programs on local communities when economies of scale are seen to be insubstantial—

elementary education might be an example. Two, public transport should be strengthened to provide youth with physical access to the specialized services offered by central cities. Three, at least for children and young people, governmental enforcement of geographic entitlement to public services should be abandoned whenever economies of scale exist in notable degree, and, if necessary to allow orderly use of facilities, other, more rational means of rationing should be used.[18] Plainly, consideration of the economy of scale problem, along with other problems in the Tiebout model noted above, casts doubt on the utility of decentralization as the single, simple answer to the search for economic efficiency in the public sector.

The Voucher Proposals

A set of proposals intended to afford even closer fit between household tastes and educational services is the education vouchers. The essential idea is that parents be offered an entitlement or voucher representing financial value when applied to placing a child in a given school, public or private. The government would supply vouchers to parents; hence, government would continue to be a main source of *support* for schools but would no longer carry such a large degree of responsibility for their *operation*.

In this section, we shall consider the following matters: Milton Friedman's pioneer proposal; the modified voucher proposal advanced by John Coons and Stephen Sugarman; the Alum Rock public sector voucher experiment; and Henry M. Levin's general analysis of the voucher idea.

The Pioneer Voucher Proposal of Milton Friedman

Professor Milton Friedman, Department of Economics, University of Chicago, put forward his voucher proposal in 1955. The argument's basic justification is as follows:

> . . . both the imposition of a minimum required level of education and the financing of education by the state can be justified by the "neighborhood effects" (social benefits) of education. It is more difficult to justify . . . the actual administration of educational institutions by the govern-

ment, the "nationalization," as it were, of the bulk of the "education industry." The desirability of such nationalization has seldom been faced explicitly because governments have in the main financed education by paying directly the costs of running educational institutions so that this step has seemed required by the decision to subsidize education. Yet the two steps could readily be separated. Governments could require a minimum level of education which they could finance by giving parents vouchers redeemable for a specified minimum sum per child per year if spent on "approved" educational service. Parents would then be free to spend this sum *and any additional sum*, on purchasing educational services from an "approved" institution of their own choice. The educational services could be rendered by private enterprises operated for profit, or by nonprofit institutions of various kinds. The role of government could be limited to assuring that the schools meet certain minimum standards such as the inclusion of a minimum, common content in their program. . . .[19]

Friedman noted certain arguments against his plan. (1) It might be hard to provide the "common core of values deemed requisite for social stability in a democracy." Particularly, this concern stems from the possibility that "schools run by different religious groups" would instill "sets of values that are inconsistent with one another" and with the prevailing values taught in nonsectarian schools. (2) The opening up of greater choice among schools might accentuate class distinction. Friedman tended to brush this argument aside. At present, the attendance areas for particular public schools are peopled by children with similar backgrounds thanks to the stratification of residential areas. Only a very few people can manage to send their children to nonparochial private schools; this fact serves to accentuate class distinction. Then, he concluded, "The widening of the range of choice under a private system would operate to reduce both kinds of stratification."[20] (3) In some rural areas, it is practical to have only a single school. Parents cannot have the satisfaction of choice because a "natural" monopoly exists, and the school might as well be run by public authorities, the only real alternative being such a degree of state regulation—to insure that no group gets unfair treatment, for instance—that the inspectors might outnumber the inspected.

In light of these problems, Friedman modified his proposal to the following:

> The arrangement that perhaps comes closest to being justified by these considerations—at least for primary and secondary education—is a mixed one under which governments would contine to administer some schools, but parents who chose to send their children to other schools would be paid a sum equal to the estimated cost of educating a child in a government school, provided that at least this sum was spent on education in an approved school. This argument would meet the valid features of the "natural monopoly" argument, while at the same time it would permit competition to develop where it could.[21]

Public authorities would still assure that private schools met minimum standards and would administer the remaining public schools. The level of public school support would continue to be a local matter. Hence, the size of the grants per child to parents who requested them would be mainly determined at the local level.

What gains does Friedman claim for his scheme of elementary and secondary education? (1) Parents would have a wider range of choice of schools for their children. (2) The greater amount of private enterprise in education would—through competition—act to make the schools more efficient and to promote a healthy variety of schools. (3) Educational enterprise would become more flexible— in particular, salaries of teachers would become more responsive to market forces.

As we noted in discussing Tiebout's analysis of resource allocations, even when the local public sector is designed to afford choice (i.e., when local districts are numerous and when they display substantial diversity in program offerings), public operation, combined with limited, high-cost, and unsubsidized private education, can *at best* offer only a cumbersome process to channel increments of household income into the purchase of a higher quality of educational services. The family that earns a few hundred extra dollars of income cannot ordinarily afford to move its residence into a town that has a high-grade school system, nor does an extra few hundred dollars buy a place for a child in a nonsecular private school. Friedman's scheme would allow a family to move up in small steps. For example, assume the dollar value of the education voucher is $1,000. Let a family have a child in a school charging $1,200—the family contributes $200. Suppose the family receives an increase in disposable income of $1,000, and imagine that it wishes to allocate one-fourth of the increment to schooling. In Friedman's educational world, it should be easy to find a school charging $1,450 a year—the family now contributes $450 (i.e., the original $200 plus one-fourth of the $1,000 increment in income). All this assumes, of course, that a student incurs the costs for himself in moving from one school to another. It would be better if the family could purchase additional educational services within the same school setting, without having to transfer the child.

What of the compulsory expenditures on education? It is hard to see that they would be any less than they are under the present system. All parents and prospective parents would have a financial stake in seeing that school levies were kept at a reasonably high level. Some parents who had formerly been lukewarm about raising school taxes because they did not like some features of the public school program would now have every reason to support the levies wholeheartedly: With the grant plus any necessary voluntary contribution, they could send their children to a nonpublic school more to their liking. Likewise, those who had formerly borne the entire expense of private education would become supporters of the school levy.

Friedman attacks the schools in terms of two values that are almost sacred in our society: consumer choice and efficiency in production. To gain (in his terms) a larger volume of private and social benefits from education, he does not eliminate public support, but rather supplements it by private funds. He does not eliminate public operation, but allows it to exist side by side with private operation.

Are there counter-arguments to the Friedman proposal? We think there are. The compelling argument for maintaining the present pattern of public operation we believe, is found in the idea of social mobility. In this country, cynicism aside, there is a devotion to the ideals of equality of opportunity and equality of status. The ideal that every child should have an equal start in life is impossible of close attainment, but the public schools have been the major instrumentality for moving as far as we have toward that goal. The justification for public operation of the schools rests, then, on the contribution of the public school system in preserving social mobility. Let us look at the point more closely.

Under a mixed system of education, the public schools would operate at a lower level of support than a large number of private schools. Yet both public and private schools would compete in the same market for teachers' services. As teachers' salaries increased, the public schools would almost certainly resort to noticeably larger class sizes. By this conveniently measurable criterion, the reputation of the public schools would suffer. Also, the public schools would almost certainly be the "dumping ground" for "problem" children. In fact, since the private schools would be in competition with each other, one could expect them to select their pupils (and staff) with the greatest care, the reputation of educational institutions depending so strongly on the human materials with which they are able to work. Public schools would be viewed as the refuge of the slow or the troublesome child—and of the very poor child.[22] It is hard to see how the public schools could escape falling into ill repute.

Among the private schools, it is claimed, substantial diversity would appear as the factor of consumer choice came to be expressed. The initial search for diversity in kind or type of program and method of instruction could come to be subsumed under a search for diversity in *quality*, real or imaginary. The effects on the students could well be more significant than the real differences in quality of schools would indicate. This is to say that the student would react not only to the quality of education he was offered but to people's opinion of his school, whether it was public or private. Those who attended the less-favored schools would feel that they had been given a poor start and might refuse to try for the harder tasks for which their innate ability would qualify them.

What degree of choice does the voucher plan afford to working-class parents? Such parents would have little means to supplement the value of vouchers by private payment. Those living in school districts of low assessed valuation would receive vouchers of small dollar value, moreover. Partly, then, the answer depends on whether low-cost diversified private institutions could develop or whether poor families would be limited to public institutions.

Let us take the favorable view and say that there would be private schools to which poor parents could send their children. One of the advantages claimed for the voucher plan is that it would increase technological efficiency in education—that is, schools would come to provide more learning per dollar because of competitive market pressures. The most effective (and, relatively speaking, easiest) action for a private school under competitive pressure is not to fire bad teachers but bad students. This is true because of the powerful effect of external economies in production of school services. This is the case even in the public sector, where dismissal is closely controlled. How much greater it would be in the private sector. Not only would disruptive, slow-learning children be got out of the way—no longer to distract the other students or to lower their norms of attainment—but the threat of dismissal would be a major incentive for the remaining students to work hard.

Would dismissal power fall on children of different classes differentially? It would seem likely, for working-class children frequently appear slow and disruptive until they come to feel at home in a given school environment. Accordingly, the working class might be expected to take the brunt. Further, working-class parents would probably be less able to protest effectively against a school management or against a teacher.[23] It would be unfortunate if the poor had their choices constrained to a local public school, probably one that had been drained of a large share of its academically superior teachers and students, at the same time that the middle and upper classes were being given new powers to guide the destinies of their children.

Family Power Equalizing

In the form of a statute drafted for consideration by state legislatures, John E. Coons and Stephen D. Sugarman unveiled an alternative to the Friedman voucher plan in 1971.[24] Called "family power equalizing" or "FPE," the Coons-Sugarman proposal is intended to cleanse the Friedman plan of the charge that it would accentuate social stratification in our country. That is, FPE seeks to preserve the attributes that are designed to offer greater household choice in education and to stimulate competition among schools; at the same time, FPE hopes that our present system's emphasis on equal educational opportunity can be maintained—or even enhanced.

How does FPE build an egalitarian focus into the concept of vouchers? First, FPE stipulates that schools entitled to accept vouchers must operate without benefit of financial endowment. If private schools were allowed to use income from old endowments or to accumulate new endowments to help support their programs, then obviously they could maintain advantages over the public schools.

Second, FPE specifies that schools must be financed strictly by the money they obtain as voucher reimbursement. Parents, that is, are not to be allowed to "add on" private supplements to the voucher entitlements they receive from government. This represents a substantial departure from the Friedman plan, and it seems to require specification of school expenditure limits corresponding to voucher values. Letting schools A through D represent public and E through H private, Coons and Sugarman illustrated that idea by proposing the following expenditure limits:

TABLE II
SUPPORT LEVEL PER STUDENT OF FOUR LEVELS
OF PUBLIC AND PRIVATE SCHOOLS

	A and E Schools	B and F Schools	C and G Schools	D and H Schools
K-8 (equivalent)	$600	$ 900	$1,200	$1,500
High School (equivalent)	$900	$1,200	$1,500	$1,800

SOURCE: *Ibid.*, p. 13.

Third, in order to assure that families in lower income classes can select high-expenditure schools for their children, FPE specifies a scheme of finance under which the household contribution is regulated by two factors: expenditure level of school chosen *and* level of household income. Under FPE, local taxation for schools as we now know it would be abolished (it is retained under Friedman), and in its place would be substituted a kind of tax— or price for education—laid on families with children. A suggested form of such tax is the following:

TABLE III
TAX RATE BY CATEGORY OF SCHOOL TO BE
PAID BY HOUSEHOLDS OF DIFFERING
INCOMES RECEIVING VOUCHERS

Adjusted Gross Household Income	Category of School			
	A and E	B and F	C and G	D and H
0-$3,500	$5	$10	$15	$20
$3,500-$12,000	$5 + 2.3% above $3,500	$10 + 3.5% above $3,500	$15 + 5.1% above $3,500	$20 + 6.9% above $3,500
$12,000 and up	$200 + 3.0% above $12,000	$310 + 4.2% above $12,000	$450 + 5.8% above $12,000	$610 + 7.6% above $12,000

SOURCE: *Ibid*, p. 98.

In order to reduce the likelihood that rich families will choose wholly private schools (and FPE clearly assumes their continued existence), the plan specifies that no family shall pay an amount of school tax in excess of one and one-half times the sum of all the amounts credited to tuition accounts by reason of school attendance by all the children for whom a taxpayer is responsible. For rich families, but probably *only* for the rich, school taxes might then vary by size of family.

These provisions are one way to define a price, and, given that we are dealing with a subsidized activity characterized both by external economies in production and by external economies in consumption, it is a rational way.[25] Classical public finance theory shows that the quality of public sector goods can hardly be expected to satisfy anyone. Most people will want either more or less of the given goods or services. The voting mechanism at best is intended to determine a single level of output for a certain service provided by a certain government that is tolerably inoffensive to the majority. Coons and Sugarman make this point: Why not cater to differences of taste within the public sector, at least for services like education where, first, external economies in consumption dictate that we cannot leave minimum levels entirely in parents' hands and, second, where parents, willy nilly, are going to intervene on matters affecting their progeny? The trick is to arrange that their intervention is not dysfunctional with respect to the external economies of production. This means that in the future parents come to accept more mixing of the social classes in schools and in school programs.[26]

The fourth device employed to undergird the egalitarian nature of FPE is randomization of admissions. Whenever a school is oversubscribed, admissions are to be guided by the process of random selection, and those students who fail to be selected are channelled to the next school that most nearly meets the parents' preferences. The main exception to random selection is the provision that prior years' students are given preference to continue in the same school; this exception is required to afford necessary stability in the school enrollment of a given family.

How well could FPE serve the objective of getting a closer fit between the educational outputs of schools? In part, the answer depends on one's subjective view of education processes and institutions. No doubt, educators exist who feel that substantial variety can be provided within a single institution—this notion is fundamental to the strong support given in America to the "comprehensive school." If this view is correct, then the variety represented by differences in expenditure level (which is to say differences in generalized quality) is all the additional variety one can ask for, and FPE *might* do the trick.

However, there are those, the author included, who feel that within-school variety of programs is no substitute for between-school differences. In other words, what we may want to have is greater specialization by type of institution rather than just by quality of institution. Take the example of instruction in the arts. A teacher of painting in a comprehensive high school, unless it is so large that four or five full-time faculty members are found in the fine arts department, is bound to feel lonely in the professional sense and is likely to regard himself as no more than an ornament to the "regular" programs. Further, only the most common arts will be treated in a comprehensive school: drama, painting, band, orchestra, but not ballet, sculpture, chamber music, Oriental music, African music, calligraphy, poetry writing, playwriting, mime, etc., except in a fleeting and nonprofessional way. Yet, creative talent blooms early in youth, and its flowering, more than in the case of verbal skills, would be no respecter of classes. A high school of creative arts would offer economy of scale in laying before youth the range of aesthetic expressions; staff members would reinforce and stimulate each other; and the administration could reasonably set standards of professional knowledge—as well as of teaching skills and of maintenance of discipline—to regulate staff advancement.

The same case for specialization by type of high school could be made in such fields as mathematics/pure science, mathematics/applied science (technology), social science, commerce, construction trades, machine trades, and languages (including computer languages). It could well be that one of the roots of student unrest is the vacuity of courses in the last years of high school and the first year or two of college. The underlying reason for the malaise may be that we delay too long the specialization necessary to serve a student's aptitude and stimulate his interests.

It might appear that FPE would be conducive to the development of such a necessary degree of specialization. A difficulty is open admissions. Once a student is entered in a school, he is not easily moved, so an initial improper sorting will have lasting effects. Since external economies of production are important in education, the actual standard of work done in what might appear to be specialized schools would become general. Specialization of program—and all the benefits that might flow from such specialization—may require admissions standards, differentiated, of course, by the particular emphasis of a given school. This would probably yield quantitatively less race and class integration than FPE with its open admissions, but there could well be more class and racial tolerance. After all, it doesn't accomplish much to have blacks and whites in the same school if most of the whites are in the college preparatory program and most of the blacks are in the shop. Under specialization, whites and blacks with similar strong interests would have a chance to work side by side.

A better solution might be to rely on school advertising and guidance to improve initial student (parental) choice and then to allow a one-year tryout for any student who is sufficiently determined and confident to enroll himself. This would reduce reliance on one-shot tests to screen applicants, which is generally a risky business anyway.

FPE leaves us with choice in terms of expenditure (= quality) but not necessarily much in terms of type of program. This is likely to be a greater degree of real choice than decentralization (alone) would give, and it is provided in a much fairer way than under Friedman vouchers. However, we are relying to a greater degree than at present on parental choice and less on the judgments of professional educators, school boards, state legislatures, the Congress, etc., to make decisions about the kind and quality of school services that should be laid before a given student. We all now recognize that different students "require" different amounts of educational resources, and that programs for the deprived, the handicapped, and the vocationally minded are relatively expensive. Better knowledge of education production functions should some day guide us to make more sensible and sophisticated expenditure differentials. Can parental judgment do as well in allocating students to programs as the professionals and public authorities? No one knows, and no one can know until we have some experimental program of the FPE type.

Finally, as the author has noted,

> . . . it is not immediately obvious that both the goals of removing the influence of household income on the quality of educational opportunity *and* offering notably greater freedom of choice in the selection of educational programs can be obtained. Tying those two objectives together creates an incongruity—becoming more egalitarian and at the same time serving differences in consumer preferences more precisely. Traditionally, when a public program is attacked, as public education is now being attacked, on the grounds that it is distributing its services in a discriminatory manner, the response has been to make services more uniform—to reduce differences in what is offered to different groups of households.

> The solution that is proposed under FPE is ingenious and deserves extremely careful study. Actually, the FPE treads a narrow path, and at the risk of being obvious it should be pointed out why the path is narrow. Until now it has been assumed that all choices in education that people want to make are good and socially helpful. Most might be, but perhaps some people would use their new options to undermine major national values. For example, some might exercise the opportunity granted under FPE

to create a new type of elitist and white separatist institution. There are a number of provisions to forestall the possibility of this happening. Three of these we have noted are: the proscription of using income to build an endowment, the disallowance of parental supplements to stated tuition rates through extra fees paid directly from their household income, and random selection of students in cases where a given school is over-subscribed. The critics of the FPE contend that these controls are not sufficient. It may be pointed out for example that controls on teacher selection are modest and, therefore, a school could establish criteria (of teacher recruitment) which discouraged application from the poor or the blacks (as students). It might also be said that since the Act does not proscribe the compulsory wearing of uniforms by students, the poor could be discouraged by a school's establishing such a requirement.

Thus, the dilemma is presented: Controls are necessary, because otherwise too many people might make anti-social choices. On the other hand, the more comprehensive and detailed the controls become, the less chance there is of obtaining any real diversity in types of educational institutions. It is pointless to give people the right to choose unless diversity exists—stringent control of private schools, for example, with respect to the kinds of faculty they must hire would tend to negate alternatives which would otherwise be presented. The control problem is, then, the crux of the matter.[27]

The Alum Rock Voucher Experiment

Stemming from work done by the Center for the Study of Public Policy in Cambridge, Mass., the Office of Economic Opportunity, and later the National Institute of Education provided substantial funding toward an experiment with educational vouchers in the Alum Rock Union School District, San Jose, Calif.[28] The district serves approximately 15,000 students through eighth grade in a predominantly Mexican-American area of the city.

Initially, OEO intended that the experiment involve both public and private schools, that school revenue depend entirely on enrollment, that students hold rights of transfer from one school to another at any time, and that no guarantee of survival would be offered to any school when voucher income failed to cover expenses. Students would gain admission to a school of their choice on the basis of a lottery. Student transport would be provided as a matter of public expense. School "fees" were to be limited to the value of a basic voucher, equal in dollar value to the district's current spending per student. An extra "compensatory" voucher would be provided to poor children to allow additional services to be provided for them. The original idea stressed very strongly the objective of affording choice to students and their parents and the fostering of competition among schools.

As accepted by the Alum Rock Union School District, the plan actually implemented involved public schools only. Indeed, in the first year of operation (1972-73), only six of 24 public schools of the district joined the experiment. Choice was expanded, however, by providing that each participating school would offer at least two distinct programs, called "mini-schools." The second main departure from the original OEO plan was to provide that teachers' job tenure and seniority rights were guaranteed. The upshot is that the final arrangement did not provide as much competition as had originally been intended.[29]

In the 1973-74 school year, the number of voucher schools increased from six to thirteen. Parents and students were offered 43 different programs, ranging from "traditional plus" through "bilingual-bicultural" and "individualized learning" to "math-science" and "fine arts." On a form prepared in English and Spanish, parents were requested to indicate their first three choices of program. Parents were provided with a one-page statement of description for each of the 43 programs.[30] In addition, many meetings were held to discuss which schools might best serve the interests of the children of a given parent. Students were assigned to programs by lottery whenever programs were oversubscribed; however, in certain instances, popular programs were expanded to serve all clients, using space in underenrolled buildings or portables. All schools had some form of parent advisory council.

Though the Alum Rock plan provided only limited competition among schools, and though individual schools were under informal pressure not to experiment in such an extreme fashion that work assignments of teachers were substantially altered (as might occur, for example, if large numbers of paraprofessionals were substituted for certificated persons), this venture, nevertheless, is a bold experiment in the decentralization of decision making. Faculties came to have considerably more power over curricular decisions than they ordinarily do. Asking parents to think a bit about what kind of school programs would best fit their children is certainly a commendable step for a local authority to take.

The first year's results of the Alum Rock experiment were assessed by the Rand Corporation. Their chief findings were the following:

1. Given the incentive of federal funding . . . Alum Rock was able to decentralize decision making to the school level and offer parents a choice among instructional programs, without stirring up disruptive conflicts within the community. . . .
2. The real changes in Alum Rock may flow from the creation of mini-schools in each school. The mini-schools offer what parents perceive to be a genuine choice at the neighborhood school level. . . .
3. Because mini-schools are small . . . certain time-honored values of the American school system are being reintroduced: children and teachers work together over a period of years, and older and younger children are grouped together. . . .
4. On the whole, parents and teachers, when surveyed, are reasonably well satisfied with the demonstration. . . .
5. . . . data on student outcomes . . . were inconclusive or absent. . . .
6. The fears of voucher critics that parent choice would result in increasing segregation by race or social class were not borne out. . . .[31]

Henry M. Levin's Summary Assessment of Vouchers

For a number of years, Professor Henry M. Levin of Stanford University has been studying the probable implications of establishing a system of voucher education in the United States. His summary views as of mid-1974 might be stated as follows.

First, defining private benefits of education as higher future earnings, enhanced social status, etc., Levin is inclined to the view that vouchers would increase private benefits, at least for members of the middle class.[32] He suggests that competition among schools would lead to increased effectiveness in their operations. Schools would adopt more "imaginative" recruitment policies and would be inclined to heighten financial incentives in order to encourage teachers to work hard. (Presently, most teachers in public schools are paid primarily under a seniority system, so hard work doesn't necessarily get one a bigger salary as long as one remains in the job of teaching.) Schools would be more likely to ". . . adopt a policy of flexible class size depending on subject matter, grade level, and type of student, which is a more sensible goal than maintaining uniform class sizes."[33]

Second, Levin defines the social benefits of education as those which accrue (1) as the country achieves a minimum level of literacy, knowledge, and common values among all members of the population, and (2) as the country reduces disparities in income, status, etc., that are related to race and social class. He concludes that a voucher system would impinge negatively on the flow of social benefits as defined. Levin gives several reasons for his pessimistic assessment; here, we cite the following:

(1) Admitting that public schools do not well serve residents of low-income neighborhoods and that public schools often fail to establish minimum standards of literacy, knowledge, etc., Levin nevertheless concludes that the quality of education provided the poor under a market orientation would be even worse.

. . . while the private market would likely provide many educational alternatives to middle-class children, there would probably be far fewer sellers of educational services to the children of the poor. It is important to note that schooling must be consumed at the point of purchase; therefore, geographical location of schools becomes a salient feature of the market place. But if the previous experience of the slums can be used for prediction, few if any sellers of high quality educational services at competitive rates will locate in the ghetto. Not only is there no Saks Fifth Avenue in Harlem; there is no Macy's, Gimbels, Korvetts, or Kleins.[34]

(2) Admitting that public schools are characterized by a high degree of social class isolation, Levin notes that it is nevertheless true that ". . . there are at least some poor children in middle-class schools and some middle-class children in working-class schools."[35] This situation is likely to be worsened under vouchers, to the extent that social class isolation is increased.

If parents choose those school environments that they believe will maximize the probability of success as defined within the context of their experience, the working-class child will be provided with schooling that will reinforce working-class orientations while children from higher classes will attend schools that will orient them toward the upper echelon of the occupational hierarchy.[36]

The effects of such systematic differences in educational environment, based on social class, will help perpetuate a largely static class structure from one generation to the next. But this is not the end of the story.

Though the voucher mechanism will serve inherently to expand the present inequalities, it is the victims who will be blamed for making poor choices. Under such circumstances we will lose one of the few readily identifiable focal points of institutional culpability, the schools, as a visible cause of the social disability of the poor; for under vouchers the responsibility for obtaining the appropriate education for succeeding in life will rest on individual families rather than on society.[37]

Other Possibilities to Increase
Consumer Choice in Education

We have seen that "voting with one's feet," Tiebout style, is a cumbersome means of providing consumer choice in education. Furthermore, under our local system of government, the opportunities for families to match public services with their own particular preferences are quite unevenly distributed among income classes: As under any known market arrangement, the rich enjoy greater opportunities than the poor. Vouchers allow closer fit between services obtained and perceived private benefits. However, voucher systems are subject to attack on the grounds that they fail to give us a due return from education in the form of social benefits and that they are likely to increase social stratification in the society. Are there more preferable means of affording households choice with respect to educational services? We think there are.

Diversified Offerings of Local School Districts

Whether or not the Alum Rock experiment is a true voucher scheme, it is certainly a program that offers parents and students a chance to select among a diversified set of educational environments. Many school districts do not offer such variety of choice—but some do! In Berkeley, Calif., 22 alternative educational programs were available in 1972-73. A number were housed in buildings specially leased for the purpose—"found space." There was a school of the arts; a program organized around environmental studies; a "black house"; an intense college preparatory program, "geared for students who can or need to do better"; and various programs that emphasize interaction among students and between students and teachers.[38]

Both Alum Rock and Berkeley are middle-sized school districts. Can large city districts offer similar kinds of choices? Apparently the answer is affirmative. Minneapolis and Milwaukee allow students and their parents to select schools outside their normal intra-city attendance areas. New York and, to a degree, Boston, have long been known for their specialized high schools. The point is that much more choice than we now see can be offered within the public sector in a manner that does not require the use of vouchers and does not require households to change residence in order to obtain a different type of educational service.

Provision of Specialized Instructional Services by Regional Authorities

In the nature of the case, almost all schools (except for large high schools such as New Trier) find it impossible to offer highly specialized services to students. Where in a typical K-12 school program does one find in-depth treatment of physical anthropology, astronomy, ballet, Oriental languages, Eastern music, or even geology? On the physical side, how many schools provide rowing, riding, or soccer? In the absence of a method of serving specialized tastes, one might contend that students who want such things should wait until college to get them, but this view fails to take into account the facts that many students do not attend college and that if students' desires are not served when they are most intense, interest may vanish forever.

Fortunately, there is a way to serve specialized interests in a relatively inexpensive fashion—through developing a set of regionalized institutions to enroll students in the hours when they are not in regular school: afternoons, evenings, weekends, and summers. Student enrollment would be voluntary, of course. We see voluntary participation as the only workable and fair form of rationing specialized instructional services. No agency public or private, can make available to each student what all other students might like to have for their development and pleasure. But if the obligation extends to providing expensive things only to those who are seriously interested, and if the client population is sufficiently large to afford thorough utilization of specialized goods and services, the problem is solved. For example, suppose in a high school of 1,000 students, there are 10—1 percent—who are keenly interested in astronomy. Unless it is unimaginably rich—or is a university training school—there is no way the school can justify the purchase of a large telescope, cameras, darkroom, and the time of a Ph.D. in astronomy (even on a part-time basis). Now, imagine that a regional educational authority is established to serve a population of 50,000 students, of whom 25,000 are of an age to want to spend time in an observatory. If the 1 percent proportion of interested persons holds, there are now 250 clients for the service. The regional authority can justify a service to these 250 students. Meeting in groups of 25 for two hours each week, they would establish an astronomy demand in the regional center for 20 hours of instruction per week. Given that this demand should be more or less permanent, it could justify purchase of modest equipment and the part-time services of fully trained astronomers. Not even voucher plans can provide the degree of curricular choice that lies within the grasp of regional authorities in all of our metropolitan areas (though there is nothing inconsistent between the establishment of a voucher scheme *and* the further development of regional education authorities).

Among the large nations of the world, USSR has explored most fully the potential of regional educational centers. As in our case, whether in secondary general education or in secondary vocational/technical education, students tend to follow a rather uniform pattern of learning in their hours of formal schooling and to leave school at a more or less fixed time—approximately 17 to 18 years of age. However, Soviet authorities recognize that some students have special interests, aptitudes, and talents that require identification and nurture. Accordingly, the "Young Pioneers" learning agency operates in parallel to the formal school. The centers of supplementary instruction are sometimes called "Pioneer Palaces."

> Pioneer Palaces may now be found throughout all of Central Asia. The facilities, however, vary greatly from rural to urban settings. In some of the larger population centers, Tashkent, Samarkand, Bukhara—the Palaces

border on elegance. In rural areas the Pioneers generally use the school facilities.[39]

Programs are characterized by extraordinary variety. Science is emphasized: Physics, chemistry, marine biology, electronics, space, astronomy, and geology laboratory facilities abound. Much attention is given to art: Music, drama, ballet, painting in all its forms, sculpting, and writing facilities and programs are to be found in the palaces. Hobby and craft exercises are available: photography, weaving, radio, gymnastics, model building, and the like. The palaces allow for deployment of highly specialized instructional staff and facilities and benefit from economies of scale.

It must be emphasized that participation in programs of the palaces is voluntary. Hence, an underlying theme of the whole program is service to individuality.

> Youth leaders appear to place a high priority on developing special interests and talents, and some youth programs are organized to serve talented youth only. However, the neighborhood palaces are for all who wish to participate, and they cater to a wide range of interests and talents.[40]

Regular progress in the formal school program brings rewards in the form of access to the activities of the Pioneer Palaces.

To assure that voluntary participation is not only a feasible but a fair form of rationing, access to programs must be unrelated to such irrelevant variables as parental income, race, or location of home. The latter requirement implies a system of cheap public transport for students in junior and senior high who lack private means. If voluntary participation can be freed of such irrelevant controlling variables as income, class, etc., then students would "purchase" specialized instructional services by offering to spend their time in receiving such services. No social class divisions are implied in this plan, as they seem to be in the major voucher programs. Choice would be granted, but on the basis of intense common interest in a subject of study or play. These conditions could well bring groups of different class and ethnic backgrounds more closely together than ever before.

Greater Specialization in Instructional Capability

Catering to students' specialized instructional interests, whether in a conventional school district or in a regional educational authority, requires that at least some teachers come to perform in a more highly specialized way. One solution to the problem is the employment of part-time teachers.

No amount of restructuring of the assignments and responsibilities of teachers is going to make full-time classroom teaching attractive to all persons. Thus the problem of attracting teachers with diverse backgrounds and interests is a persistent one. We believe that greater use of persons willing to teach part-time would introduce diversity in staff, heighten vitality in school programs, and present students with greater choice in the activities they pursue. Fortunately, different types of people can be potential part-time teachers.

College and University Faculty

It is now well known that graduate institutions are producing more Ph.D.'s than the job markets can possibly absorb in full-time employment. If public schools could employ such persons on a part-time basis, all parties would benefit. College and university faculty members might be used in public schools in several ways:

Persons who serve on faculties of four-year colleges and universities are ideally suited, at least in terms of their knowledge of subject matter, to lead classes for the most academically talented students in a school. Such part-time arrangements would permit students to make contact with those who work at the forefront of knowledge in particular areas of study and to develop and enlarge their interests in highly specialized fields. We think it a cheerful prospect that students beginning their own periods of greatest intellectual curiosity and agility might have access to the best academic minds available.

Faculty on loan from colleges and universities should be used by individual schools or school districts to conduct seminars for elementary and secondary teachers. Teachers are more likely to take advantage of academic instruction if it is offered in their own school district than if it is offered at a more distant and impersonal university. Also, if all or most teachers of a given subject in a school or school district attended the same seminar, we would expect that the common experience would stimulate teachers to develop new and interesting proposals for additional courses to be offered in their schools, or for changes in emphasis in existing courses. In any event, increased intellectual vitality should be an objective of all schools, and we believe that the addition of highly trained people from colleges and universities would serve to increase such vitality.

In fields that require rigorous analytical thought such as mathematics, physics, chemistry, and economics, any teacher is likely to have an imperfect understanding of some points of analysis. A public school teacher may be unaware of a new theoretical development or uncertain about its implications. It is not always possible for such a teacher to clear up the difficulty by attending evening classes at a university or by taking summer courses. The topic may not be treated in sufficient detail, and the teacher may be embarrassed to ask questions that reveal a lack of understanding. It would therefore be profitable for part-time staff members on loan from a college or university to make time available for individual consultations with teachers in their respective districts. In a less formal atmosphere, the teachers could explain their problems and receive help. They could gain confidence and willingness to engage in serious academic discourse with their brighter students.

Craftsmen, Artisans, and Skilled Workers

Students are extremely curious about the larger adult world. The ordinary school teacher is often unable to provide information about the actual nature of various work activities. Hence we propose that small categorical grants be used by school districts to attract craftsmen and skilled workers for part-time service in schools. These people would have a threefold role in the school: (1) to meet with interested groups of students to discuss the important characteristics of manual trades, including working conditions, unionization, grievance procedures, and promotion leaders; (2) to conduct classes in their trades; and (3) to counsel students about opportunities in the labor market for workers without college training. It would be useful to encourage businessmen to play a similar role in the schools.

Technicians from Fields of Unusual Interest

As a complement to part-time teaching by artisans, craftsmen, and skilled workers, we think it desirable that students be in touch with people involved in unusual technical trades, as for example, weather forecasters, air traffic controllers, computer programmers, and international news reporters. These persons would not be inclined to accept any regular employment in a school district, even part-time, but we urge districts to make an effort to bring them into schools for short visits.

Lawyers

Many adults have serious misconceptions about their legal rights and responsibilities and generally possess little awareness of the basic principles of jurisprudence. There is firsthand evidence that high school students are very interested in knowing more about the law. Existing courses in history, civics, and political science could be supplemented to great effect by the part-time employment of practicing attorneys with firsthand knowledge of legal processes. To some extent, their services might be made available *pro bono publico*.

Artists, Musicians, and Actors

Students with actual or latent interest in aesthetic fields would be immensely stimulated by contact with painters, sculptors, calligraphers, and related professionals in the field of visual arts. Those interested in music, acting, and dance would surely benefit from the opportunity to talk with and take occasional lessons from a successful practitioner of one of the performing arts. The extraordinary success of "Sesame Street" indicates that performers often make instruction more pleasant and its results more successful. The accomplished actor or musician invigorates a classroom in ways beyond the imagination of most regular teachers.

Housewives

Countless married women have had advanced training in academic fields or experience in the performing or visual arts. We are certain that many of these women, if not burdened with the responsibilities of full-time teaching, would be interested in working in the schools. Wishing to give priority to their households, they may seek to avoid full-time assignments and the obligation that acceptance of a full-time salary would impose. On the other hand, they desire to use their knowledge and skills. Women outside the labor force can be a valuable resource for American education.

Thus, there are ways to offer a choice of programs, and the list could presumably be extended. They are not inconsistent with localism in supply of educational services nor with vouchers, but they go beyond both in the range of choice to be made.

CHAPTER III

The Grand Search for Technological Efficiency in Education

As we noted earlier, economic efficiency rises as producers fit their products ever more closely to the preferences of consumers; on the other hand, technological efficiency rises as producers find and utilize the least costly combinations of inputs to produce certain defined outputs. Technological efficiency has nothing to say about whether consumers prefer—or should receive—higher quality goods or services. Hence, if we say that school districts should pay attention to the question of how to provide educational services cheaply, we could at the same time contend on grounds of economic efficiency that households should be provided with educational services of high quality. In short, technological efficiency is a matter of avoiding waste, with the idea that the resources saved have important alternative uses. The 1960s were a time of considerable confidence in the ability of local education authorities, using findings of various research ventures, to achieve markedly higher standards of technological efficiency. In the first half of the 1970s, considerable disillusionment has set in. The truth probably lies between the optimism of the 1960s and the rather extreme pessimism of the present time.

Yet, analysis of educational resource allocations is an important matter. The economist discusses allocation of resources with the purpose of constructing an analytical apparatus to derive the criteria of efficient schemes of production. A normative goal in economics *is* efficiency in production. Education occupies a strategic place in productivity advance. On the one hand, it enhances the strength of the work force in both private and public economies. This contribution could be recognized even if technology were static. But major gains in productivity are commonly associated with change, i.e., improvements in technology. A necessary condition for improvement in technology is the activity of scientific research. Clearly, the quality of future scientists' education is crucial in determining the value of the new knowledge they will finally offer to society. Let us call these kinds of outcome the "indirect contribution" of education to productivity.

In contrast, improvement in efficiency *within* the public school system can be defined as "direct contribution," similar to the direct contribution that can be made by any private or public activity. As compared with the general run of economic activities, it is important to be especially concerned with education in terms of its internal productivity relationships. We noted in Chapter I that education is our "largest industry." Under a national policy of promoting greater efficiency in production, it makes sense to give special attention to large users of resources. More importantly, any improvements in educational efficiency are extended through the rest of the economy because of the activity's indirect contributions. Under a national policy of promoting economic advance, it is wise to stress the use of better techniques in those lines of work that *do* offer an indirect contribution, in contrast to those that do not (such as the manufacture of razor blades or chewing gum). Further, any deficiencies in quality of education will affect the society for a long period of time—especially as man's life span is extended. The potential value of the skilled worker and the scientist alike may be lost to society when the individuals receive an inadequate education.

In spite of economists' interest in technological efficiency, it does not follow that they possess a generalized theory of production. For example, they make comparisons among a large number of school districts in an attempt to assess whether districts that employ disproportionately large numbers of highly experienced teachers display higher standards of student achievement. By controlling for the influence of other variables that affect the given output measure (i.e., student achievement), economists would feel qualified to establish a relationship between teacher experience and educational output. They would proceed similarly, using the same or different output measures, to assess the relative contributions of other inputs. But they do not operate from a theory of learning, which is to say that they do not pretend to know *why* teacher experience, for example, affects student achievement. Economists would function in a similar way if they were assessing the contributions of different productive agents in a shoe factory.

Present concern with policy analysis in the public sector stems basically from the recognition of certain deficiencies in decision making. These might be listed as follows:

(1) The objectives of public programs often are not translated from broad generalities into operational (quantifiably measurable) terms; hence, program accomplishments are frequently not well considered.

(2) Where program review is made, on the other hand, it is concentrated in too short a period of time.

(3) Budget analysis generally centers on expansions and new services, and thus commonly fails to examine the continued worth of old programs; further, operating and capital budgets are seldom fully integrated.

(4) Alternative means of accomplishing given ends are not presented for consideration of chief administrative officers, along with those cost-effective analyses that allow efficient choices among means to be made.

(5) Future costs of present decisions are not described in a thorough and systematic fashion.[1]

If these criticisms apply to budget preparation in school districts, how have school budgets actually been prepared? Mainly, it seems, by extending last year's budget into the present, modifying it somewhat to take account of new state and federal categorical grants, changes in the hiring price of teachers, the prices of instructional materials, etc. This, of course, is not a method that produces a careful weighing of educational priorities or assures maximum yield from the district's educational resources.

Can nothing be done to improve the process of resource allocation? Obviously so, if there is will to do it. We now consider a rational approach: program budgeting, sometimes called the planning-programming-budgeting-system (PPBS). We shall also describe two major analytical exercises, cost-effectiveness analysis and estimation of educational production functions. Both of these two analytical exercises are intended to provide information for the successful implementation of program budgeting.

The Concept and Application
of Program Budgeting

Interest in the application of scientific techniques to budgetary decisions in education may be said to stem from work of economists and systems analysts of the late 1950s and early 1960s. Joseph A. Kershaw and Roland N. McKean of Rand Corporation prepared a report in 1959, entitled *Systems Analysis and Education*. This report suggested that it was not only desirable but possible for school districts to compare the marginal benefits of one type of expenditure over another and to merge the benefit comparison with cost estimates to choose the budgetary option that gave the most return for the dollar spent.[2] At about the same time, Kenneth Deitch of Harvard said that educational administrators should make use of "marginal return calculations" in deciding how to assess preferred budgetary choices. He suggested that they should provide themselves with three major kinds of information: the objectives of the agency and their relative importance; the variables the administrator can control and those he cannot; and the relationships between controllable variables and achievement of important objectives. With such knowledge, administrators could relate returns from different variables to each dollar of expenditure and reach an equilibrium that maximized output in the allocation of the agency's resources.[3]

The process, then, is deliberately to establish in the public sector an equivalent to the competitive pressure that forces firms in private markets to discover the least-cost means of achieving given output. If competitive pressures in private markets are strong enough, we can be reasonably sure that firms will discover—and employ—efficient means of production; if no more scientific basis is available for assaying the relative efficiencies of different approaches to production, then trial and error will do. In the public sector, not only are competitive pressures generally absent, but outputs are hard to measure because the complete nature of outcomes is not revealed until many years have elapsed. Program budgeting is the main effort so far established consciously and deliberately to direct public agencies to allocate resources in ways that minimize the costs of accomplishing given ends. What are the steps of program budgeting?

First, program budgeting ". . . calls for the careful identification and examination of goals and objectives in each major area of governmental activity."[4] A second step is to analyze the present output of a program in terms of its objectives.

> For example, the effectiveness of various manpower programs can only be determined in relation to a particular set of objectives. "Creaming off" the manpower pool by concentrating training resources on unemployed white high school graduates may prove highly effective when measured by the proportion of trainees subsequently employed at steady jobs and higher wages. But if the objective is to improve the lot of the hard-core unemployed . . .

in the ghetto . . . such measures of effectiveness would be inappropriate and misleading.[5]

A third step is measurement of costs of alternative programs. A fourth, and most crucial step is

. . . the analysis of alternatives to find the most effective means of reaching basic objectives, and to achieve these objectives for the least cost.[6]

PPBS was developed in a special part of the public sector—the military. Even though military analysts never succeeded in establishing an operational definition of "military worth," PPBS had become a well-accepted process of analysis in the Defense Department by the early 1960s.[7] On the assumption that whatever worked in defense would work anywhere, President Lyndon Johnson announced in 1965 that PPBS would be implemented throughout the federal government.

The enthusiasm for PPBS at the federal level, however, was quite short lived. By 1969, the Joint Economic Committee of the U.S. Congress was receiving testimony to the following effect:

In the three and a half years since the system (PPBS) was instituted, analytic staffs have been created, program structures have been defined, and program memoranda and financial plans have been presented. Despite adherence to the formalities of the system, however, the predicted solution has not taken place. Presentations purporting to be analyses are often no more than poetic rewording of old style budget submissions. Where attempts have been made to present real calculations of costs and output, the conclusions have been rejected on the grounds of political irrelevance.[8]

The sharp reversal of attitude at the federal level dampened efforts to apply PPBS in local government, including school districts.

Given that PPBS appears to be an eminently rational approach to the problem of efficient resource allocation in the public sector, what went wrong? A major difficulty is that PPBS was vastly oversold. It was presented as if detailed scientific analysis alone could guide us to correct policy conclusions. In other words, value judgments, on which it is often so hard to reach consensus, could be dispensed with. Unfortunately, nothing in the PPBS apparatus offers guidance for weighing the significance of one major objective against another.[9] As William Gorham, a leading advocate of PPBS and formerly Assistant Secretary (Program Coordination), U.S. Department of Health, Education, and Welfare, said in testimony before Congress,

> Let me hasten to point out that we have not attempted any grandiose cost-benefit analysis designed to reveal whether the total benefits from an additional million dollars spent on health programs would be higher or lower than from an additional million spent on education and welfare. If I was ever naive enough to think this sort of analysis possible, I no longer am.[10]

Secondly, the PPBS experience at the federal level assumed that widespread, comprehensive adoption of the system was feasible and that this new framework for allocating resources in the public sector could be set in place quickly. Neither assumption was justified. Opportunities for high-grade, rigorous policy analysis differ markedly from one agency to the next. In highway and water resource projects, assessment of costs and returns is relatively easy; in health, education, and recreation, they are relatively difficult. A given department's capacity to implement PPBS varies, depending upon whether the department has a confluence of talented analysts, a scarce breed. The attempt to force a rapid introduction of PPBS caused civil servants to do what most of them knew they could not do well; thus, they understandably viewed PPBS with cynicism.

Two other difficulties should be mentioned.

> . . . PPBS assumes a flexibility that is frequently not present in public bureaucracies. When the acceptance of PPBS necessitates some radical changes in the methods of providing a service, those whose status or jobs are threatened can be expected to thwart the shift, even while proclaiming the worth of the new ideas. Such persons can use various means to prevent change in public service; assigning

work according to seniority is the most easily noted . . .
(next) PPBS assures the acquiescence of public interest
groups affected by major changes in the provision of services. Once a group has become accustomed to being
taken care of by the operation of any program, it rarely
wants to yield its favored position to increase the technological efficiency of the service for the whole population. Affected public interest groups are likely to use political influence to see that . . . changes recommended by advocates
of PPBS are not implemented.[11]

However, there is much to be said for PPBS, both in
terms of its present usefulness and in terms of its potential as a system of administration. As Charles L. Schultze,
former director of the federal budget has stated,

The most frustrating aspect of public life is not the inabil-
ity to convince others of the merits of a cherished project
or policy. Rather, it is the endless hours spent on policy
discussions in which the irrelevant issues have not been
separated from the relevant, in which ascertainable facts
and relationships have not been investigated but are the
subject of noted debate, in which consideration of alternatives is impossible because only one proposal has been developed, and, above all, discussions in which nobility of
aim is presumed to determine effectiveness of program.[12]

Imperfect as its application has been, PPBS has served to
lower these kinds of frustrations.

For one thing, it has stimulated efforts to clarify objectives in public agencies. In the health field, for example,
instead of speaking of "providing adequate care to all,"
one is more likely to specify, for example, that infant mor-
tality in a given area of a city be reduced by X percent
in a stated number of years.[13] In education, the statement
of a general objective, like providing for the full intellectual development of each child, is nowadays often accompanied by more precisely phrased queries, such as the
following: Assuming that a certain sum will be available
as incremental resources, how should these resources be
distributed among different types of students? At what
points in the educational career of different types of stu-

dents—pre-school, elementary, junior high, or secondary—
should incremental resources be concentrated, in order to
improve ultimate opportunities for learning?

The more systematic analysis of resource allocations that
PPBS in principle implies has been associated with general
improvements in budget documents. A standard school district of a few years back might show a format for the function of instruction as follows:

Instruction
    Teachers' salaries $ . . .
    Noncertificated personnel salaries   . . .
    Textbooks   . . .
    Other materials of instruction   . . .
                              Total $ . . .

Presently, one is more likely to find instructional budgets
broken down to reveal expenditure by level of school program and by type of instruction offered. For example, one
segment of a new-type school budget might read as follows:

100 Instruction—Reading
    01 Developmental reading, total $ . . .
       001 Elementary school services   . . .
       0001 Personal services   . . .
       0002 Supplies   . . .
       0003 Capital outlay   . . .
       002 Junior high services   . . .
       0001 Personal services   . . .
       0002 Supplies   . . .
       0003 Capital outlay   . . .
       003 Senior high services   . . .
       0001 Personal services   . . .
       0002 Supplies   . . .
       0003 Capital outlay   . . .
    02 Remedial reading, total, etc. $ . . .

This type of budget format, indicating in much greater
detail the distribution of resources by specific functions of
the schools, allows administrators and other interested
parties to see how flows of funds to particular programs

have changed over time and, hence, to ask why the flows have changed in some special manner—or perhaps why flows have *not* changed in the light of announced objectives of the districts or in the face of facts known about special needs of certain students. It has been suggested, furthermore, that budgets that display functional detail should be prepared by individual schools.[14]

Individual school budgets could have important uses. Whenever students in a school were failing to meet expected standards of performance, either in conventional types of learning or extracurricular fields, those who had an interest in that school should be able to make a case for extra funding to help overcome its deficiencies and, equally important, to determine whether the school received extra assistance relative to funding levels of other schools of the district. Presumably, allocations of budget within single schools should bear a relationship either to the instructional philosophy of the school or to the characteristics of its students—or both. The availability of single school budgets should allow school boards and district administrators to see if differences in spending patterns among schools existed, and, if so, whether the differences appeared to be rational.

Lastly, interest in PPBS has served to stimulate policy analysis. An example is the development of "simulation models" in education.[15] Simulation models are sets of equations, commonly placed in a computer, that allow educational administrators to ask "what if" questions. For example: With respect to school district costs and local tax rate, what if enrollment falls at a rate 10 percent faster than first expected? What if the ratio of students to professional personnel at the junior high level is increased by 2 at the same time it is reduced by 3 in the primary grades? What if we go to a plan of year-round operation of schools? The essential ingredients of a simulation model are enrollment projections by grade, ratios of students to teachers by grade, teachers' salaries, building space per student, and various specialized cost estimates. Simulation models can be extremely useful to administrators in examining the cost consequences of teachers' demands in the collective negotiations process and in preparing counter proposals on the employer's side.

Cost-Effectiveness Analysis

Cost-effectiveness analysis is an essential component of PPBS, in that PPBS implies examination of alternative means to accomplish given ends *and* the selection of a preferred alternative on cost criteria. Actually, cost-effectiveness studies in education are limited in number, in part because of the difficulties of describing educational outcomes and inputs rigorously and in part because economists have been interested, at least until recently, in the more ambitious task of analyzing "education production functions." (We shall consider production functions in the next section.)

First, let us draw a distinction between "cost-benefit studies," otherwise known in education as "returns to education studies," and "cost-effectiveness." Cost-benefit studies seek to answer the question of whether a given activity is worth undertaking, in the light of alternative opportunities to invest resources. Taking account of the cost of preventing students from dropping out of high school, on the one hand, and the extra lifetime income that high school graduates earn compared with dropouts, cost-benefit analysis asks whether a dropout prevention program is worth what it costs.[16]

Cost-effectiveness analysis, on the other hand, is concerned with determining which means are preferred to accomplish given objectives. Suppose that an objective is stated as "raising the level of interest of primary school students in music." One means is to send regular classroom teachers back to school to study music more thoroughly; another is to employ music specialist teachers to work with each class of primary school students a few hours a week; another is to employ professional musicians to teach on a part-time basis; yet another is to send the students out to hear rehearsals, performances, etc.; finally, one might establish a "music lab" in which many instruments were available, along with tape recorders, etc., for the students to use and experiment with. Cost-effectiveness analysis would seek to demonstrate which of these alternative means gave the largest increase in students' interest in music for the dollar spent.

Stating the nature of cost-effectiveness analysis in this way displays the difficulty of conducting such investigations. One difficulty is defining outcomes. In measuring musical interest, there are no widely used standardized tests available. Even if there were, arguments would crop up about their relevance, for plainly, "interest of primary students in music" means different things to different people. Is it more important that most children come to like music more (and what kind: Mozart, Bernstein, rock, African drums?) or that a few children become aware that they have real musical talent? In the face of such difficulty, cost-effectiveness analysis is commonly confined to the more easily measured educational outputs—ordinary reading skills, say, as measured by standardized achievement tests.

But music is important, too, so let us stay with that example. Assume that some measure of interest in music is used by a large number of school districts. The analysis would proceed by trying to find districts that had a program of inservice education in music for primary school teachers, one that used specialist teachers of music, and so on. The costs (average) of using the different means would be reckoned. Finally, the *costs* of the alternative means would be related to *levels* of musical interest. Plans where costs were high relative to student interest levels would be ranked low in cost-effectiveness terms; where student response was high relative to costs, a given program might be recommended for adoption in additional school districts.

In this instance, measurement of costs would pose a problem. Inservice training of teachers in music is a kind of capital investment. To obtain annual costs, comparable to costs of hiring specialist teachers for a year's service, we would need to amortize the inservice training outlay over a stated number of years. The number of years would be a function of teacher turnover in the district, and teacher turnover is often hard to predict.

More important, data drawn from the experience of large numbers of school districts, expressed as some sort of average value, are not closely representative of any single school district; nor are they a clear guide to what a single district that embarks on a particular course of action will experience. For example, success of teacher retraining in music may be strongly related to the teachers' previous knowledge and interest in music as well as to these teachers' incentives to improve their instruction in music. Data on these points are not easily recognized in cost-effectiveness studies, so whether another district will experience success from a similar investment of resources is problematical. Likewise, the success of a program of employing specialized teachers in music, relative to cost, would probably depend on the competence of the specialists engaged and their interest in working with the particular sorts of students of the district. Teaching of music, after all, when done successfully, carries a considerable emotional interchange between teacher and student, and the kinds of data commonly fed into cost-effectiveness do not easily deal with the chemistry of teacher-student emotional reactions.[17]

Nevertheless, cost-effectiveness analysis is occasionally a useful venture. As an example, consider Henry M. Levin's analysis of teacher recruitment.[18] Using data from the Coleman Report (see discussion in the next section of this chapter), Levin was able to demonstrate, *inter alia*, that whereas both the verbal ability of teachers and the experience of teachers affected performance of sixth-grade students on a standardized verbal achievement score, the effect of an additional unit of teacher verbal score raised the white students' verbal score by an average of .179 points, while the effect of an additional year of teacher experience brought up the students' average score by only .06 points. That is, in terms of the scales by which teachers' verbal ability and experience were measured, teachers' verbal ability had a stronger influence on student performance.

Next, Levin examined the costs of hiring teachers in relation to the two teacher attributes. Actually, of course, the salary schedules used by school districts do not relate pay directly to the verbal ability of teachers, only to experience and training, but it is to be expected that teachers with higher verbal scores will have better marks in their college courses, better recommendations, etc., and so find their way in disproportionate numbers to districts that offer higher salaries in general. By regression analysis, Levin showed that the costs of an additional year of experience—$79 on the average—was, nevertheless, considerably greater than the cost of an additional point on the teacher's verbal score—$24.[19]

Putting these sets of findings together, Levin computed the relative costs of increasing a student's verbal score by one point was some 10 times greater by means of hiring more experienced teachers than it was by means of hiring teachers with higher verbal ability. As Levin states,

> The over-riding implication of this analysis is that school salary policy should provide financial incentives that will attract and retain teachers with greater verbal skills, a policy that would represent a distinct break from tradition. On the other hand, it is suggested that schools grant too large a reward for experience. The result of reducing salary increments for experience and implementing them for verbal performance would appear to attract a more capable teaching staff with regard to the production of student achievement.[20]

Not all cost-effectiveness analysis in education need deal with student achievement. Consider the objective of reducing the disparity of earned income between white and black workers. Until recently, available evidence indicated that education was *not* a likely route for blacks to achieve a higher degree of income equality. It had been reported that

> A non-white youth with no schooling will receive 81 percent of the income of a similar white. Yet, for non-whites,

school attendance increases income at a rate which is only 28 percent of its corresponding increase for whites.[21]

However, Finis Welch demonstrates in a recent paper that such pessimism about the utility of education for blacks in the marketplace is no longer well-founded.[22] In the first place, he was able to show that the quality of schooling available to blacks has been going up and has been improving more markedly for blacks than for whites. Second, by making comparisons between the data of the 1960 *Census of Population* and a special federal *Survey of Economic Opportunity,* 1966, Welch demonstrated that the earnings of young blacks with little work experience exceeded by a considerable margin what earlier cohorts of blacks had been able to obtain. Since the improvement in quality of black education would affect only recent entrants to the work force, the data about larger-than-expected earnings of young blacks suggest that education *is* an appropriate increase of economic advancement for minority population.

> More recent entrants into the workforce enjoy higher returns to schooling than do those persons schooled in an earlier period. Further, this upward trend is stronger for blacks, such that the percentage contribution of schooling to earnings is larger than for whites in comparing persons who entered the labor force in the 1960's but is significantly lower for those who entered in the 1930's and 1940's.[23]

Studies of Educational Resource Allocations

A basic idea in economics is that outputs of an economic activity can be provided under different conditions of production. For example, certain types of learnings may be developed by having a few highly trained teachers work with large groups of students or by having several adults, each with lower levels of training, working side-by-side with small groups of students. The former approach would be "training intensive," and the latter, "labor intensive." The general idea is that there is no single way to accomplish a given objective.

If we assume that there is more than one way to accomplish given objectives, then we may legitimately ask whether some schemes of production are to be preferred over others. The general criterion of technological efficiency is to prefer schemes that consume the least resources to provide the stated outcomes, because the resources that are saved can be put to important alternative uses. The search for greater technological efficiency in education has spawned a particular type of study called "analysis of education production functions." These studies are considerably more comprehensive than the cost-effectiveness investigations we described in the last section.

In 1964, the author was requested by the then Chairman of the Senate Finance Committee, California Senator George Miller, to provide the Senate with impartial advice on how to distribute educational funds.[24] The interested parties noted that about $2 billion of state resources were being paid out as grants to school districts, and that education interest groups made frequent requests for new, larger appropriations for school districts; indeed, the requests were a regular feature of each legislative session. The Senate felt it lacked the guidance to direct funds toward or away from different local authorities, i.e., toward or away from high-wealth districts, low-wealth districts, towns of the great agriculture valley, isolated rural districts, or large cities. California legislation provided that a minimum percentage of a district's budget be spent on teachers' salaries; at the same time, California's average class size was about the largest in the nation. The Senate wanted advice on the relative priority of concern it should display toward further advances in teachers' pay as against reduction in class size. The state held a virtual monopoly of textbooks, and the Senate wished to know whether the level of funding for texts and instructional supplies was adequate. In short, the Senate wanted to know whether it was directing its grants correctly in the geographic sense (e.g., rural districts vs. cities) and whether it should assume a more active role in controlling functional allocations of resources (teachers' salaries vs. class size, for example).

The author discovered that it was possible to obtain a great deal of information about school districts—the socio-economic characteristics of students, size and location of district, professional staffing, expenditures for different types of school inputs, etc. He also found that California had recently instituted a statewide testing program, showing achievement of students in reading and mathematics. Once access to those various kinds of data were obtained, they were fed into a computer to observe the relationship between student achievement (dependent variables) and student characteristics, district characteristics, and, especially important, expenditure and staffing patterns (all regarded as independent variables). Standard techniques of multiple regression, including stepwise regression, were used.

What did we hope to find out? Given the research setting, we obviously sought to inform education policy makers in California. For example, if we had found a positive relationship between student achievement and district size, presumably we could have argued that the state should intensify its efforts to consolidate its many hundreds of small school districts. If we had discovered that the relationship between expenditures per student and achievement was relatively strong in rural districts and relatively weak in the suburban districts, we might have argued that the state concentrate increments to its grant program in the agricultural areas, at least for the time being. The idea would have been that the marginal return to the state's educational dollar, as measured by student achievement, was greater in the rather poor agricultural population, as compared with the marginal return in the suburbs, where additions to budget might more likely to be devoted to "frills." If we had discovered a strong relationship between class size and achievement, compared with a weak one between average teachers' salary and student performance, we might have urged the state to make incentive grants to districts to obtain a reduction in class size.

Actually, we obtained no clear evidence on any of these

policy-related points. The problem was that the socio-economic characteristics of students appeared to account for practically all the variation in student performance. We could show statistical significance for school—as distinct from student—variables only with respect to characteristics of teachers. Interestingly, the relationship was reasonably strong in low-wealth and high-wealth districts, but comparatively weak in middle-wealth areas.

Shortly after the California study was underway, the U.S. Office of Education began a much larger, better financed, and better publicized project—the "Coleman Report."[25] The basic techniques of the two studies were similar, and so were the reported results: Differences in student performance are attributable primarily to the circumstances in which the students are growing up, not to differences in educational provision. Following the Coleman Report, a large number of other efforts were made to understand the effects on students of differences in school environment, and the sophistication of the statistical techniques has been raised considerably.[26] Yet, we still lack scientific evidence to guide educational resource allocations for the betterment of student learning. As noted in a major assessment of educational effectiveness studies conducted by the Rand Corporation for the President's Commission on School Finance, "Research has not identified a variant of the existing system that is consistently related to students' educational outcomes."[27]

Education production function studies have concluded that schools have little or no influence on students, that it is not very important whether students attend school or not, and that it is a matter of relative indifference how much money is spent on schools (except to those persons who find employment therein).[28] These views are contested in a recent reanalysis of the Coleman data. Speaking of cases where schooling had been interrupted over a period of time, the report states,

It was found that the children whose schooling had been interrupted exhibited severe educational retardation, particularly on tests more closely related to school curriculums such as spelling and arithmetic. On an intelligence test the scores of these children were 15 to 30 points lower than those of the children in the adjacent county who had continued in school. Clearly, the schools do have important influences. Just as clearly, one of the goals in improving the schools must be to increase the influence they have on their students that is independent of the students' social background—their educational influence, in short.[29]

What it has not been possible to do is to isolate the independent influence of school variables on student achievement. The failure is probably related to data inadequacies. Educational outcomes are not adequately measured by standardized achievement tests in reading and mathematics. On the input side, quality of teaching is surely an important variable *a priori*, but quality of teaching is described by such variables as teachers' pay or scores on a self-administered verbal test. Moreover, quality teaching for one student (or group of students) may be bad teaching for other students. Most education production function studies measure inputs and outputs at a given point of time, which is to say that they do not attempt to trace the progress of a student over a period of years, relative to the educational experience he has accumulated. Given that both students and teachers are highly mobile, and given that a set of students may be responding more strongly to their previous educational experiences than to their current ones at a given point of time, the failure to employ longitudinal data may be a serious handicap in analyzing educational production.[30]

Another problem is that persons who conduct education production function studies lack training in educational psychology and often lack knowledge of how work in a typical classroom is carried forward. Possibly teams of researchers, including not only economists and sociologists, who have done most of this kind of work to date, but also educational psychologists and classroom teachers might be more successful. The matter of the classroom teacher's responsibility to engage in applied research is the subject of the next section.

Teachers and the Improvement of
Technological Efficiency

The basic shortcoming of educational research is that little knowledge accumulates and stands the test of replication. A series of experiments in learning processes seldom show the same results when repeated in new situations, even when the situations are apparently quite similar. The recent history of educational practice is strewn with examples of bright proposals that have failed to live up to their initial promise—team teaching, the ungraded classroom, the open classroom, discovery learning, new math, instructional television—though each of these practices still has its advocates. Even the effects of such a long-established practice as tracking students remain in dispute, and doctoral dissertations continue to be written on the subject. In the face of the fact that many apparently normal children fail to learn to read, there is little hard evidence to prescribe an effective reading program for a given group of children. Among other things, education helps develop students' capacity to understand basic ideas of scientific inquiry, and it helps some students eventually to engage in scientific research of the most rigorous type, but education has failed to develop the means to analyze its own processes. What has been said in the previous sections about the rather limited results obtained from program budgeting, cost-effectiveness analysis, and education production function studies is evidence on the point. Prospects for real advance from any of these lines of inquiry as they have presently been conducted are not, in my opinion, favorable.

A peculiarity of the education service is that the main body of professionals, classroom teachers, are not involved in any large way in applied research with regard to the services they offer. The papers read at the annual meetings of the American Educational Research Association, for example, are written mainly by faculty members in colleges and universities. Such persons often lack the class-room teachers' close knowledge about how children appear to learn. Almost certainly, they lack the commitment of the serious public school teachers to build a better learning environment for the students in their charge, for the academic's commitments are to his scholarly profession, his institution of higher education, and his own career. Though there is a relationship between these latter objectives and the improvement of educational practices in the classroom, the relationship, to say the least, is not immediate and personal.

The author has long speculated on the question of how the knowledge and wisdom of the classroom teacher could be applied more effectively toward development of a more scientific basis for resource allocations in the field. We all know that teachers have at best only a limited amount of time and energy for research. We all know that many teachers are unable to express interest in the development of their profession and find complete commitment to work within their own classroom. But these same conditions applied earlier—as they still do today—to the field of medicine, in that many practicing doctors felt they had neither time, energy, nor interest in writing papers for their local medical societies.

Medical research today is highly organized and centered in teaching hospitals, research institutes, and scientific laboratories of various kinds. But it began in a more humble way, through the willingness of *some* doctors to record their experiences in dealing with patients and to read their findings to monthly meetings of their fellow practitioners. The general idea was to describe the condition of the patient when first seen, to explain in detail the treatment given, and to note the patient's later condition. It was neither necessary nor appropriate to claim casuality between treatment and results, for many doctors were searching for new, effective treatment and writing up results. But when several doctors reported similar findings, a major paper on the topic might be read at a state or national meeting of M.D.'s

The process of reporting treatment and results did not alone establish a basis for medical advance, but it did help to lay a groundwork, and it did help establish in practitioners of medicine the idea that they were partly responsible for advances in the state of their art. The complementary process of research in the early days of medical advance took place in the teaching hospital, an institution that combined the functions of applied research (sometimes using ideas from papers published by practitioners in the field), high-grade medical service to the community (given free to families of low income), and practical training for new doctors.

By analogy, education may need to develop similar processes if we are to make steady progress in developing a knowledge base for what we do in the classroom. One step is for teachers to make the effort to record their experiences and to state inferences about learning processes—and to present findings and observations in a more or less formal setting to their fellow teachers. Another is to establish in central areas a set of superior educational institutions (I have suggested they be called "professional schools"), which would have tri-partite responsibility for applied research, high-grade instruction of school-age students (drawn mainly, though not exclusively, from the surrounding and presumably low-income neighborhood), and practical instruction of new graduates who seek to enter the profession.[31]

Staff could consist in part of "clinical professors" seconded from universities and trained in such fields as psychology, sociology, pediatrics, and instructional media. The professional schools should also be staffed with teachers who had demonstrated unusual competence in instruction of the young. The long-term objective of creating such institutions would be to accumulate knowledge about what instructional practices work well with different types of students. In the shorter run, one would hope that education of central city youth would be improved and, especially important, that prospective teachers would have better opportunities to gain experience than is provided by existing programs of practice teaching and that they would have a more gradual and fulfilling introduction to sole and full-time responsibility for a classroom.

It may be noted that this proposal differs in some crucial respects from the "university school" as it is now typically operated. At present, the university school offers academic enrichment, in the fashion of the English direct-grant grammar school, to children of university faculty and other academically motivated parents. Its enrollment is not concentrated in children of the typical central city neighborhood, even though it may be located in a low-income neighborhood. Academic faculty are drawn mainly from the department of education of the sponsoring university; only rarely is a university faculty member engaged who has no appointment in the sponsoring university. This situation tends to limit the staff's research interests and to make it, perhaps, excessively academic. Finally, there is little opportunity for the staff to draw upon ideas from the field, because at present teachers have not had the will to report findings or have not developed the institutional mechanisms to channel their observations to centers of research.

CHAPTER IV

A More Perfect System
of Educational Finance

This chapter will deal directly with current issues of education finance. Before we launch into that subject, let us draw together the observations we have made in the previous chapters, for the subject of public finance of education is closely related to the points made earlier.

In Chapter I, we noted that elementary and secondary education is a very large enterprise in our economy and that the services provided in our schools undergird in important ways the economic, social, and cultural progress of our nation. Such attributes allow one to make a strong surmise that the system of education finance is properly subject to close scrutiny. If imperfections in the mechanisms of finance too harshly constrain the capacity of the education system to sustain our economic, social, and cultural growth, then we need to consider whether those imperfections can be eliminated.

The subjects of Chapter II are somewhat more complex. Presently, a large amount of administrative and financial power is held by school districts in nearly all of our 50 states. The chief economic justification (though,

as we shall see below, not the only justification) for localism in the control of educational services is to afford
choice to households in the selection of schools for their
children. Localism instills a measure of market choice in
the public sector, in that by deciding to live in a school
district, or in a neighborhood, the family opts for the services of a particular set of teachers, working in a particular center of learning. The process of choice is similar to
that under which a housewife in a supermarket chooses
steak as a main dish for dinner instead of canned baked
beans.

Like exercise of market choice in the private sector,
choice within the public sector, up to the present time at
least, has reflected the prevailing income distribution. The
richer a family is, the more choice it has, and the richer
a family is, the higher the quality of goods and services
it expects to consume. So it is, by and large, with schools.
Rich families tend to seek out suburbs populated mainly
by other rich families; such suburbs generally have well-
financed schools, which are at the same time institutions
of academically superior standards. Or rich families settle
in those parts of large cities that have high residential
property values and send their children to schools from
which low-income children are excluded by local attendance boundaries. Or rich parents in big cities use private
schools.[1] Rights of school attendance are basically a matter
of geographic entitlement. To get better schools, a family
must be able to move into an area in which the better
schools are located. It is obvious that the richer households are more able to seize such opportunities, as those
opportunities require the means to be geographically
mobile *and* the means to afford high-priced housing.

In Chapter II, we noted that considerable interest has
been expressed in extending the degree to which households can select educational services for their children by
issuing educational vouchers. Such economists as Milton
Friedman defend voucher proposals on the grounds that,
because tastes differ among households, any reasonable
way to expand choice *ipso facto* heightens the total well-

being of the country. Another defense of voucher proposals is that education voucher systems will make schools more competitive, meaning, *inter alia,* that teachers will work harder, with the result that the output of educational services per dollar spent will increase. Legal scholars such as John Coons see vouchers as a means to provide poor families with the same measure of choice in educational services that rich families already have. In any case, the general effect of adoption of education voucher schemes is to make the distribution of educational services conform more to *market principles* than to *state control.* It would also presumably increase the decision-making power of the individual family *vis-a-vis* government with respect to schools. My own conclusions about the voucher issue—and the reader may disagree—are these. First, vouchers would increase the degree of social stratification in our schools even beyond what it is today. Whether learning of standard subjects would be reduced, I cannot judge, but the opportunity of children from different home backgrounds to get to know each other definitely would be lessened, and I would regard this as a loss. Second, as far as curricular choice is concerned (educationally the central decision a household should be interested in), substantial opportunities are already available to enlarge it *within the public sector.* Some of them were noted in Chapter II. It would seem appropriate to explore these opportunities before adopting voucher systems, given the probability that vouchers carry the price of greater social stratification. So I conclude, finally, that public control over provision of educational services should not give way to exercise of control by individual families acting on their own behalf and as separate from the process of voting on state and local educational issues.

Chapter III appeared to open a new topic of discussion—technological efficiency in education—but its relevance to the previous argument will now become clear. If we are not to rely upon the market to record our educational decisions and direct the flow of educational resources therefrom—if instead we look to government to regulate type, quality, and distribution of services—it would be highly desirable if government could garner scientific information to guide its resource allocations, to help determine, that is, *where* to place incremental resources, on *which children* to concentrate incremental resources, and *by what means* funds could best be employed to achieve desired end results. The general point of Chapter III is that such scientific information is not yet available, in spite of the fact that many dedicated scholars over the last decade and a half have tried to help produce it. Furthermore, it seems that scientifically based findings to inform education policy decisions are not likely to be forthcoming in the near future.

Enter the courts on the issue of education finance. As is well known, the courts in a number of states have ruled that the existing system of education finance discriminates against poor people or—at the best—distributes educational resources in an irrational fashion. The general order of remedy is for state governments to play a more active role in educational resource allocations (though some of the more popular reform schemes would leave considerable discretionary powers over spending at the local level, as long as the state acts to equalize local taxing power). Thus, a fundamental dilemma is posed: Our state governments are charged to reform school finance at the very time when earlier hopes for evidence to support rational allocations have been rather effectively squashed. If state governments take strong action to equalize educational expenditures among districts, or if they embark on programs to support services for students who have special needs, they do so without evidence to justify the details of their policies. If they do nothing and leave things as they are, they are charged with violating the constitutional rights of families to equal education. It is not a comfortable era for educational policy makers nor their clients.

Past Distribution of Educational Resources

In Chapter I, we saw that approximately 90 percent of school district revenues are obtained from state and local government. Local revenues are drawn primarily from property taxation. For the most part, property tax yields are obtained from levies on "real property:" owner-occupied houses, apartment houses, hotels, factories, warehouses, stores of all kinds, and land. The property tax rate can conveniently be thought of as a percentage levy, for example, a "$4.00 per $100" property tax rate means that taxes in the current year are 4 percent of the *assessed value* of the property. Assessed value is presumed to bear a relationship to the sale value of the property in the market, and by conventional practices properties are assessed at some fraction of their presumed true or sale value. A house, for example, may be assessed at 25 percent of its market value, so a "$4.00 per $100" school tax rate is actually a tax rate equal to 1 percent of market value. Assessment ratios are supposed to be the same for different pieces of property, at least those in the same class (e.g., houses vs. factories), and those situated in a given taxing jurisdiction.

The state's portion of public school support, averaging about 40 percent of total school revenues nationwide, is commonly distributed in its main part under an arrangement called the "foundation program plan." The basic ideas are simple. The state government estimates an annual dollar cost of providing an adequate education to a child. The cost of the foundation program in a given school district is the product of the number of public school children it has to educate and the dollar value of the foundation program amount. For example, if a district has 1,000 children in its public schools, and if the state has set the value (or cost) of the foundation program at $1,000, then the total foundation program expenditure in the district is 1,000 x $1,000 = $1 million. The state government does not normally expect to meet the entire cost of the foundation program from its own state revenue sources. It specifies that local school districts levy a tax on assessed value of their taxable property to help meet at least part of the bill for the total cost of the foundation program. Suppose the assessed value of property *per student* in the district noted above was $10,000. Total assessed value in the district would be 1,000 x $10,000 or $10 million. Let the state require the districts to levy a property tax at 4.0 percent to make a "fair local contribution" toward costs of the foundation program budget. This would yield $400,000, leaving $600,000 to be supplied by the state. A poorer district would receive a larger grant and a richer district a smaller one, but the procedure employed by state governments assures that each district can provide an "adequate" education for each child at a tax rate no higher than that specified as representing the "fair local contribution." Ordinarily, the foundation program plan has only one value though sometimes states would post a higher value for secondary students than elementary. Ordinarily only one tax rate is specified to represent the "fair local contribution."

Under certain circumstances, the foundation program could (would) work quite well. First, there should be no major differences in prices that school districts have to pay for teachers' services, instructional materials, schoolhouses, maintenance, etc., as one moved from one part of the state to the other. Second, districts would need to be large enough to include more or less equal proportions of children who are costly to educate, or some action would be required to see that even small districts had no more than their proper share of costly children—children requiring, say, bilingual teachers. Third, the local taxable resources per student would need to be more or less uniform among the districts of the state.

It was particularly the failure of the system to meet this last—and easily measurable—criterion that attracted the ire of the courts. Recall the school district described just above of 1,000 students, situated in a state with a foundation program plan under which the foundation program's cost per student is set at $1,000 and the local property tax contribution rate is set at $4.00 per $100 of assessed taxable property. We assumed that the amount of taxable property per student was $10,000. Putting all the figures together, we see that the district can spend $1,000 per

student a year by levying a local tax at the standard contribution rate, $4.00 per $100, raising $400,000 locally
and receiving a grant of $600,000 from the state govern-
ment. These two figures yield a total budget of $1 million,
or $1,000 per student.

Imagine that an adjacent school district also has 1,000
students but that it is considerably more fortunate in local
tax base, reckoning an assessed valuation of $100,000 per
student. (Such variations in locally taxable property per
student are by no means unusual, mainly on account of
the very uneven distribution of commercial and industrial
properties.) Total tax base in the second district is 1,000
x $100,000 = $100 million. Let the second district levy a
local tax at the same rate as the first: $4.00 per $100 of
assessed valuation. The yield is $4 million, providing for
an expenditure of $4,000 per student. Both local districts,
then, exert the same "effort" to support schools, but
the second district is able to offer its students a program
four times as generous as the first district's.[2]

What generally develops under a foundation program
plan of support is that poorer districts, as measured by
the value of locally taxable property per student, have
higher local school tax rates and offer a more meager set
of services to their students than do rich districts. This is
contrary to the demands of equity in a local government
structure, namely, that those local citizens who desire
high-priced school services for their children pay local
school taxes at relatively high rates, while those citizens
who live in a district where by common consent a lower
level of school services is acceptable obtain the offsetting
benefit of a low school tax rate.

Fiscal advantages enjoyed by some local communities
serve to enhance property values in those districts. Take
two houses of similar type, one located in the Los Angeles
Unified School District and one located in Beverly Hills.
It is probable that the Beverly Hills house will carry a
higher price tag than the Los Angeles one, in part because
of the fact that the Beverly Hills resident enjoys the twin
advantages of a low school tax rate and an extraordinar-

ily good school system.[3] (Not that the Los Angeles schools are bad, by any means, but the Beverly Hills program is unquestionably richer in its offerings.) Likewise, compare two similar apartments, one located in the City of Boston and one in Brookline, a community well known for the academic superiority of its school program. The advantage of having access to Brookline's schools would tend to raise the rental value of the Brookline apartment relative to the one in Boston.

What it all comes to is that quality of public education in America is for sale, in the same way that quality of goods in private markets is for sale. If a family wants "good schools" for its children, it must establish geographic entitlement for them to attend school in a "good district." Establishing residence in a good school district requires purchase of a relatively high-priced house or rental of a relatively high-priced apartment.

Given the fact that rental properties, especially those with more than one bedroom, are not evenly distributed in many of a country's metropolitan areas, the purchase of superior schooling, moreover, has the characteristic of lumpiness. Consider a family with three school-age children living in a district that is providing an educational program of $1,000 per child per year. Let the family be one of modest income, but let it have a rather inordinate interest in academic pursuits. Suppose there is a nearby school district that offers a substantially superior program at a cost per student of $1,500 a year (50 percent greater than the first case). If the family could agree with its resident school district to transfer the $3,000 it was spending on its children annually to the preferred school district, and if the preferred school district would accept the family's three children upon payment by the family of an additional $500 per child, thus fully covering the cost of the three extra children to the receiving district, then for an incremental payment of $1,500, the family could obtain the kind of schooling it more nearly prefers.

However, geographic entitlement operates differently and is likely to impose a larger incremental cost on the family that prefers the superior schooling. Suppose that the family lives in a house valued at $30,000 and is paying $200 a month in principal and interest on its mortgage. To move to the superior school district, assume that the cheapest house the family can find costs $80,000. Even if equity in the old house covers the down payment, so that no "threshold" cost is attached to the move, monthly charges for principal and interest are likely to rise to approximately $550, an increase of $350 a month. Annually, the family has to pay an incremental sum of $4,200 to obtain an educational program for its three children, although the incremental school cost is, as noted, only $1,500. Many families might be able to meet the latter sum but could not accept the former. Hence, public education services appear to be rationed by income in a particularly discriminating way.

Now, let us look at the system of allocating educational resources from the perspective of a different set of parties, namely, the residents of superior school districts. These families are likely to be rather well off. Even for upper-income families these days, the value of the houses they live in—their equity, that is—is a substantial part of their estate. These families, then, do not face with equanimity the prospect of seeing their realty values sharply reduced. What kinds of events might cause values to drop in a given community? One of the main causes would be a substantial rise in local tax rates unaccompanied by an equivalent rise in quality of local services—or, worse still, the combination of higher taxes and an absolute reduction in quality of services. Because elementary and secondary education is by far the most expensive public service, and because quality of education and the amount of violent crime are major interests of prospective homebuyers, real estate values are especially sensitive to what is happening in the local education sector. Hence, people in our high-priced houses have a concern to see that newcomers to their school district do not have large numbers of children per household nor children who would add extra costs to the school budget. They are also concerned that new homes built in the district are of a type and quality that insures

that their sales prices—and hence their assessed values—
are at least equal to the prevailing standard of the community. Otherwise, average taxable value per household
will fall, and taxes will have to rise to maintain existing
standards of services. So it comes to this: The structure of
our education finance system establishes incentives for
privileged households to exclude the less privileged from
their school districts. The means utilized are various, but
zoning and covenants are two common legal expressions
of the exclusion process. The system of education finance,
thus, is one of the features of our society that promotes
social class isolation by residence.[4]

Such imperfections as these in the system of education
finance led the California Supreme Court to state in the
case of *Serrano v. Priest,*

> Although equalization aid and supplemental aid (from the
> state) temper the disparities which result from the vast
> variations in real property assessed valuation, wide varia-
> tions remain in the revenue available to individual districts
> and, consequently, in the level of educational expendi-
> tures. For example, in Los Angeles County . . . the Bald-
> win Park Unified School District expended only $577.49
> to educate each of its pupils in 1968-69; during the same
> year the Pasadena Unified School District spent $840.19
> on every student; and the Beverly Hills Unified School
> District paid out $1,231.72 per child. . . . The source of
> these disparities is unmistakable: in Baldwin Park the as-
> sessed valuation per child totaled only $3,706; in Pasa-
> dena, assessed valuation was $13,706; while in Beverly
> Hills, the corresponding figure was $50,885—a ratio of 1
> to 4 to 13. . . . Thus, the state grants are inadequate to off-
> set the inequalities inherent in a financing system based
> on widely varying local tax bases. . . . We, therefore, ar-
> rive at these conclusions. The California public school fi-
> nancing system . . . obviously touches upon a funda-
> mental interest . . . this system conditions the full entitle-
> ment to such interest on wealth, classifies its recipients
> on the basis of their collective affluence and makes the
> quality of a child's education depend upon the resources
> of his school district and ultimately upon the pocketbook

of his parents. We find that such financing system as presently constituted is not necessary to the attainment of any compelling state interest. Since it does not withstand the requisite "strict scrutiny," it denies to the plaintiffs and others similarly situated the equal protection of the laws. If the allegations of the complaint are sustained, the financial system must fall and the statutes comprising it must be found unconstitutional.

In retrial before the Los Angeles County Superior Court, the allegations of the complaint were sustained. Subject to final appeal before the California Supreme Court, the state's educational authorities have been given six years, dating from 1974, to reduce wealth-related disparities in spending among school districts to no more than $100 per student. New Jersey is similarly under court order to reform its education finance system. Approximately 60 cases on education finance of the *Serrano* type have been filed in the country, a number still pending, including a major case in New York in which property-poor suburban districts and the large cities have joined suit against the state. As we shall note later, a number of states have acted on reform of education finance even in the absence of a strict judicial order.[5]

Are there arguments in favor of the pre-reform financial arrangements, of which the most typical is the foundation program plan described above? Yes. I shall note three.

A historical argument recognizes that our country has achieved a very wide distribution of educational opportunities, even as compared with nations that approach our own in wealth. Local freedom to spend money on schools, together with acceptance of the fact that some local districts are going to have a great deal more money to spend than others, may substantially account for the fact that we have a broad-based educational system (even though its quality varies considerably from one place to another). The idea is that the richer districts would use their powers over educational policy *and* their wealth to establish secondary schools. By force of emulation, less wealthy districts would feel the need. Thus, secondary education spread widely at a time when the bill for universal secondary education (if it had had to be borne by the federal government, or even by the states) would have seemed so enormous as to be unjustifiable. As I have written earlier,

> What our country did, consciously or not, was to exploit local demands for secondary education, with the states giving to local authorities power to extend secondary schooling and at least a modest amount of financial assistance toward that end. The "high school" became a symbol of local pride and hope. But to exploit local demand means that the central authority—in this case the state government—must not raise many questions about standards. The quality of the institutions so established reflected the differences in local wealth and in the intellectual backgrounds of the local residents. The differences in quality remain remarkable even to this day, even though "universal secondary education" had become a reality by the time of World War II.[6]

It should be recognized, of course, that this argument for perpetuating disparities in provision may no longer be valid, because we have already obtained a widely extended, open elementary and secondary system. The more urgent task now may be to see that gaps in quality are closed at the same time that the overall level of quality of education is increased.

A second argument in favor of pre-reform education financial arrangements proceeds along the following lines: When a school district spends a large sum of money per student, it does so for status reasons or to provide its students with extra consumption benefits. These matters should not provoke envy on the part of neighboring districts, since they do not give special advantages to graduates of the given district in the world of work. Further, if these additional expenditures are made from tax funds raised locally, no fiscal inequity is established *vis-a-vis* residents of other school districts.[7]

I believe this argument is deficient in several respects. First, money spent to establish the status, say, of a high school, if it is spent successfully, is bound to affect favorably the prospects of its graduates in gaining admission to first-line colleges and universities. Given the fact that enrollment in such institutions is grossly biased against the poor and minorities, it would seem unwise to encourage rich local districts to exploit their taxable resources in this fashion.[8] Second, as I indicated in Chapter I, I hold that the distribution of consumption-type education among individuals is highly important and becoming more so. Third, the argument that money raised by local tax "belongs" solely to the residents of the local district is fallacious. Local authorities are created by the state governments and have no taxing powers independent of state constitutional and legislative provision. Furthermore, the inclusion within local tax bases of vastly disproportionate amounts of commercial and industrial property means that the actual geographic congruence between the amount of local taxes paid by local residents and the total amount of local taxes collected is absurdly low.

The third argument, which does, in my opinion, possess current validity, stresses that the pre-reform system of finance is highly productive of revenue for schools. As G. A. Hickrod has stated,

> . . . educators tolerate a certain amount of inequity in school expenditures as the price they pay for engaging in a game of "catch up." The rules are widely known but seldom frankly discussed. Essentially, the game proceeds by having the wealthier districts move their expenditure levels upward, and the education community places pressure on state government to assist the poorer local districts to catch up, within a reasonable distance, of the leaders.[9]

Thus, because parents in one district want their children to have as good an education as the children in a neighboring—but higher-spending district—they vote increases in taxes for schools. This is simply a process of "keeping up with the Joneses" in the public sector. But when districts' taxable resources are very uneven, the gap in spending between rich and poor districts will grow over time. From time to time the size of this gap forces the state government to raise the level of its own grants to bring low-spending districts within a reasonable distance from the rich. Thus, the structure stimulates spending at both local *and* state levels. In contemplating reform of education finance, we face, possibly, a policy tradeoff. We can maintain the present system and hope it continues to be highly productive of revenue. Or we can adopt more egalitarian systems of finance in the face of the possibility that the total amount of educational spending in a given state will be less than if reform measures had not been taken. It is even conceivable that an egalitarian system would yield a lower level of school expenditures on youth from low-income families than a nonegalitarian system would. To favor reform, the citizen should be inclined to think that *relative disparities* in provision are important. Those who oppose reform—oppose it in good will, that is—might give priority to absolute levels of spending obtained in different types of school districts.

A Digression on Progressive
and Regressive Relationships

The terms "progressive and regressive" have special meanings in the literature of public finance, and the meanings apply both to the collection of taxes and to the distribution of benefits of publicly financed programs.

On the tax side, a levy is classified as progressive if the amount of money collected from different households represents larger *shares* of household income in richer families than in poor. That is, suppose two families have annual incomes of $100,000 and $15,000. Let a tax be levied on the first household at a rate of 30 percent of income, so that it has a tax bill of $30,000, and an amount to spend or save of $70,000. Let a tax be levied on the poorer household of 10 percent, so that it pays $1,500 in tax and has $13,500 to do with as it sees fit. This is the case of a progressive tax: What matters is not that the richer family pays more dollars in tax—indeed, it would pay

more under almost *any* conscionable legal arrangement—
but that the richer household pays at a higher rate.

Under a regressive tax, the situation in shares of income
paid by rich and poor families is simply reversed. The 30
percent levy could be laid on the $15,000 family, so that
it would pay $4,500, and the 10 percent levy could be re-
quired of the richer family, so that it would pay $10,000.
Again, note that even under a regressive tax scheme, the
richer family may, and in this example does, pay a larger
absolute amount of taxes.

There is, of course, the middle case of a proportional
tax, in which all families pay exactly the same percentage
of income as tax, regardless of their income. Assume that
the two families cited above make up the whole country,
so that national income is $115,000. If the government
wanted to raise $31,500 in taxes (the sum obtained in the
first example), and if it wanted to do so under proportional
taxation, it would compute a rate as $31,500/$115,000
= 27.4 percent, and apply that rate to both households.
The richer household would pay $27,400 and the poorer
$4,100, adding up to the required $31,500.

In general, economists prefer progressive tax instruments, but their reasons may vary in accordance with
their social values. Some economists believe it is a good
thing to have a large, active public sector. To finance a
large public sector, progressive taxes, within limits, are
thought to have the advantage of political acceptability.
If big public expenditures are financed mainly by taking
large sums away from poor people, revolutionary violence
is predictable. Other economists may prefer progressive
taxation because they favor a more even pattern of income
distribution among households and they see progressive
taxation as the most politically feasible means to move
toward their objective. The most common justification for
progressive taxation is less extreme than either of the
above points of view. It starts with the premise that rich
households obtain less pleasure or utility in spending the
last dollars of their income than do the poor. It is a matter
of comparing the pleasure obtained by the rich family in

going out to dinner in an expensive restaurant with the satisfaction derived by a poor family in purchasing warm clothing for their children. The idea is enshrined in the principle of diminishing marginal utility of income. When rich families are forced to give up larger shares of income in taxes than poor, presumably, the tax collector snares a smaller number of "high utility" dollars than he would if he employed a regressive scheme of taxation. However, because of the difficulty inherent in comparing one family's satisfaction with that of another, no scientifically based scale of diminishing marginal utility of income has been established. Hence, there is no way to derive a progressive tax structure that would exactly minimize the total of dissatisfaction in giving up opportunities for private consumption summed over all households in the economy.

A second major difficulty in the design of a fair and equitable tax system is that it is very difficult to judge who is actually paying taxes. Consider the following case: A school district levies a property tax on a factory situated within its borders. The tax bill is mailed to the management of the corporation that owns the factory, and a check is drawn to the favor of the school district by the company treasurer. Obviously, the company treasurer does not see himself as paying the tax on the factory, though he signed the check. Consumers of the factory's products may actually pay the tax in the form of higher prices. People who work in the factory may pay the tax by receiving lower wages. The owners of the company, the stockholders, may be the ones who pay. The answer to this question differs from one type of business to another; it may differ in periods of economic boom and recession. All together may pay some share. So far, economists have not been able to obtain generally agreed upon answers to certain major questions in tax incidence.

This is not to conclude, however, that nothing at all can be said. Table IV presents the most recent and thoroughly compiled estimates of incidence for three major taxes: individual income, sales and excise, and property. Clearly, individual income is a progressive tax, while sales and excise levies are regressive. This indicates that insofar as school finance reform proposals offer policy advocates a choice for more intensive use of one or the other of these two tax instruments, the choice in equity terms should strongly prefer the individual income tax—federal, state, or both.

But most arguments about revenue sources in the school finance reform movement center on the property tax. Is it a good tax? Should it be used more or less intensively? Unfortunately, evidence on this important point, as shown in the table, is ambiguous. If one believes that property taxes are ultimately paid by owners of capital, which is to say that the total property tax burden is distributed among taxpayers in proportion to the amount of capital of all kinds they own, then one might conclude that the property tax is progressive and should be used more intensively to finance schools and other state-local services. If, on the other hand, one believes that property tax on apartments is passed along to renters and that property taxes on factories are passed along to consumers, then one must consider that the tax is regressive and should be phased out, if possible. Table IV shows the numerical consequences of making these alternative assumptions.

Regardless of whether one views the property tax as basically regressive, and this was the prevailing view of economists for many years, the tax is too productive of revenue to be abandoned in the short run. Rather, we should note how the equity of the tax might be improved. (In the main, the following observations could be supported under either assumption about the progressiveness/ regressiveness of the tax.) First, equity would almost be enhanced if the administration of the tax were moved from the local to the state level. Partly, this is a matter of improving administrative procedures. State-supervised administration of assessments, though not necessarily perfect in itself, results in fairer assessments of property values compared with what is handed down in many local jurisdictions. But there is more to it than simply administrative efficiency. Local property tax bases per capita (or per student) are so grossly uneven in the United States that a locally administered system cannot fail to bestow favors on some taxpayers at the expense of others. There is no underlying economic justification for the disparities. Hence, the substitution of a statewide school property tax for locally administered school property taxes is a feature often found in school finance reform plans.

TABLE IV

Effective Rates of Individual Income Tax, Sales and Excise Tax, and Property Tax, by Adjusted Family Income Class, 1966: Two Alternative Incidence Assumptions[a]

First Incidence Assumption

Adjusted Family Income ($1,000)	Individual Income Tax Percent Tax Rate	Sales and Excise Tax, Percent Tax Rate	Property Tax, Percent Tax Rate
0-3	1.4	9.4	2.5
3-5	3.1	7.4	2.7
5-10	5.8	6.5	2.0
10-15	7.6	5.8	1.7
15-20	8.7	5.2	2.0
20-25	9.2	4.6	2.6
25-30	9.3	4.0	3.7
30-50	10.4	3.4	4.5
50-100	13.4	2.4	6.2
100-500	15.3	1.5	8.2
500-1,000	14.1	1.1	9.6
1,000 and over	12.4	1.0	10.1
All Classes	8.5	5.1	3.0

[a]Under the first incidence assumption, it is held that individual income taxes are paid by individual taxpayers, that sales and excise taxes are paid by households in proportion to consumption of taxed commodities, and that property taxes are paid by owners of capital, i.e., not by renters or consumers of products of taxed capital.

Second Incidence Assumption[b]

Adjusted Family Income ($1,000)	Individual Income Tax Percent Tax Rate	Sales and Excise Tax, Percent Tax Rate	Property Tax, Percent Tax Rate
0-3	1.2	9.2	6.5
3-5	2.8	7.1	4.8
5-10	5.5	6.4	3.6
10-15	7.2	5.6	3.2
15-20	8.2	5.1	3.2
20-25	9.1	4.6	3.1
25-30	9.1	4.0	3.1
30-50	10.5	3.5	3.0
50-100	14.1	2.4	2.8
100-500	18.0	1.7	2.4
500-1,000	17.7	1.4	1.7
1,000 and over	16.6	1.3	0.8
All Classes	8.4	5.0	3.4

[b]The second incidence assumption is the same as the first with regard to income and sales and excise taxes. However, it is assumed that levies on land are paid by owners of land, that levies on shelter, including rental shelter, are paid by those who occupy the shelter, and that levies on commercial and industrial properties are paid by the consumers of the products and services of the taxed capital.

SOURCE: J. A. Pechman and B. A. Okner, *Who Bears the Tax Burden?* (Washington: The Brookings Institution, 1974), pp. 38, 59.

The second equity improvement in any given state is to adopt or expand the use of property-tax "circuit breakers." The idea is that when residential property taxes on low-income households reach a certain proportion of family income, the circuit "breaks," and additional property taxes on the particular households are forgiven. Another way to look at the idea is to say that low-income households are granted rebates when the property tax burden becomes excessive, relative to their income.[10]

Earlier, we noted that the terms "progressive" and "regressive" can be applied to the distribution of public ser-

vices as well as to the manner of revenue collection. This
topic does not fit easily within the field of modern economics, for modern economics deals best with things that
can be subject to quantitative measurement. Lacking
agreement even about what constitutes the benefits of
public sector programs, as well as about the ultimate
beneficiaries, quantitative valuations of the benefit derived
by different classes of households from different sets of
publicly financed activities has not been carried off.

The general idea, however, is that services are distributed progressively when low-income households receive a
disproportionate share of benefits and regressively when
rich households receive a disproportionate share. Title I
programs of the Elementary and Secondary Education Act,
1965, are an example of programs that are intended to
be progressive in distribution. When a city subsidizes a
marina that is enjoyed primarily by people who can afford
to own yachts, we have an example of a public program
that is regressive. What the mix should be, what the relative fiscal magnitude of progressive and regressive programs should be, is more a matter of social values than
economics.

On a slightly different point, however, economics does
have something fairly definite to say. It is a cardinal principle of public finance that government should afford
"equal treatment to equals." If a country adopts an individual income tax, for example, any two families of equal
income should pay approximately equal amounts of tax,
after recognizing legitimate differences between them with
respect to number of dependents, etc. For tax purposes,
factors of race, political persuasion, and the like are irrelevant. If two families paid different amounts of tax on account of skin color, this would represent a violation of the
principle of "equal treatment of equals."[11]

In effect, the courts have found that school finance
arrangements in several of our states violate the principle
of equal treatment of equals. Assume that two young
students of equal aptitude and interest are growing up in
adjacent school districts. Let the families of both students

be poor, so that neither family can afford to purchase private education. Assume one school district has a large tax base per student and the other a small one. We can be reasonably sure that one student will receive a much more expensive education than the other. In the absence of compelling evidence to explain the necessity for the disparity, some courts have held that the practice violates the rule of equal treatment of equals, notwithstanding absence of evidence that educational disparities are crippling.

Two Main Reform Proposals: District Power Equalizing and Full State Funding

In light of the problems so far discussed in this volume, two main proposals for reform of education finance have come forward: district power equalizing and full state assumption. We will describe each of these proposals and attempt to display their strengths and weaknesses. In the next section, we will discuss a third proposal that has not yet received much attention: district consolidation.

Neither district power equalizing nor full state funding are new proposals. A version of district power equalizing was adopted in England at the time of World War I. Henry C. Morrison of the University of Chicago was persuasively arguing that the state take over the financing of elementary and secondary education in the early 1930s.[12]

The basic ideas of district power equalizing are (1) that the state and the local school district share in providing the money that makes up the budget of the school district; (2) that the authorities of the school district, not the state, decide what the size of their budget shall be; and (3) that the state share of the locally determined school budget be greater in poor districts. This last provision is generally interpreted to mean the following: Any two districts that levy the same tax rate shall have the same amount of dollars to spend per student (excluding, of course, dollars received under categorical programs, such as compensatory education, school lunch, and the like). The "power," accordingly, that district power equalizing equalizes is the financial power of a school district to raise funds to support educational programs for its students, insofar as that power is expressed in the levy of a local school tax rate.

To see all this more clearly, consider the two school districts of our earlier example. The first district hereinafter called District A, has a tax base of $10,000 per student. The second district has a $100,000 tax base for each student—let's call it District B. Suppose the state establishes a DPE schedule under which the prescribed local tax rate for an expenditure program of $1,000 per student is $4.00 per $100 of assessed valuation. Suppose Districts A and B decide that they will have a school budget of $1,000 per student. The total budget in each district (again, excluding money received in the form of categorical aids) will be 1,000 students x $1,000 = $1 million. District A will raise $400,000 locally (4 percent of a total tax base of $10 million and will receive $600,000 from the state. District B will raise $4 million (4 percent of a total tax base of $100 million), handing over $3 million to the state for redistribution to poorer districts and keeping $1 million for its own school program. (The process of transferring property tax yield from one school district to another is called "recapture," referring to the state's claiming access to revenue generated in excessively wealthy districts. Maine and Wisconsin have recently adopted DPE plans that include provision for recapture.)

In any case, we see in our example that the three characteristics we listed for DPE are fulfilled: State and local authorities share in meeting a school budget; the size of the budget is determined locally; and the state's share is larger in poor districts than in rich.

DPE plans, formerly called percentage-equalizing arrangements, can be described in rather complicated algebraic formulas, but that is not necessary either to understand the plan or to operate it. All that is required is for the state legislature to establish a schedule under which local tax rates are related to a set of basic expenditure levels per student. One such schedule might be the following:

DPE PLAN I

Local Tax Rate Required (dollars per $100 of assessed valuation)	Basic Local Expenditure Per Student
$2.00	$ 400
3.00	700
4.00	1,000
5.00	1,300
6.00	1,600
7.00	1,900
8.00	2,100

Under DPE Plan I, any district that chose to spend $400 per student would have a local tax rate of $2.00; any district that chose to spend $1,300 per student would have a tax rate of $5.00, etc., all without regard to the size of their local tax bases. A district that contained a privately owned utility plant of large assessed value and that had few students to educate would lose its favored status, for it would now have to pay the same level of school tax rate for any given level of expenditure per student as a district that had only very limited taxable resources.

Note that DPE Plan I contains equal increments in the amount of expenditure per student for each dollar rise in local tax rate. If the state wished to encourage districts to spend a great deal of money per student, it might adopt a schedule under which expenditures rise progressively:

DPE PLAN II

Local Tax Rate Required (dollars per $100 of assessed valuation)	Basic Local Expenditure Per Student
$2.00	$ 400
3.00	800
4.00	1,300
5.00	1,900
6.00	2,600
7.00	3,400
8.00	4,500

If the state wished to discourage spending, it could specify that student outlays rise at a slower rate than required local taxes:

DPE PLAN III

Local Tax Rate Required (dollars per $100 of assessed valuation)	Basic Local Expenditure Per Student
$2.00	$ 400
3.00	700
4.00	950
5.00	1,150
6.00	1,300
7.00	1,400
8.00	1,450

Finally, the state might wish to encourage districts to spend money on educating their students up to some point—possibly considered as the appropriate level of expenditure for the typical student in a typical district (always, up to now, such "typical sums" must be judgmental) but to discourage expenditures at levels beyond that point, in order, *inter alia*, to protect the state budget. In such a case the state might adopt a schedule like the following, with a "kink" point at $1,300:

DPE PLAN IV

Local Tax Rate Required (dollars per $100 of assessed valuation)	Basic Local Expenditure Per Student
$2.00	$ 400
3.00	800
4.00	1,300
5.00	1,700
6.00	2,000
7.00	2,200
8.00	2,300

Up to the level of $1,300, adding dollars of local tax rate

allows expanding increments of spending. After $1,300, the "normal expenditure amount," additional local tax dollars yield ever smaller increments of money for schooling of students.[13]

It is well to be clear about just what district power equalizing equalizes—and what it doesn't. In choosing their educational policies, districts need no longer be concerned about the size of their locally taxable resources, in the sense that a district with a low tax base might formerly have worried that an expensive program would carry with it a local tax rate of a height almost beyond imagining.[14] But DPE does not equalize household incomes among districts, so if one district contains primarily rich households and another district contains primarily poor ones, the residents of the former district might feel better able to afford a high school tax rate than the latter. In other words, DPE does not necessarily assure a random distribution of school expenditures by income class.[15]

If DPE truly represents reform of education finance, then districts with a large tax base will have to face the prospect of paying increased tax rates for school services (while low-wealth districts will receive a tax break). Otherwise, past inequities are not overcome, and reform is empty. But the process poses difficulties for certain large cities. Both New York and San Francisco are among the wealthiest districts, in terms of tax base, in their respective states. Both cities contain large numbers of low-income families. Under DPE, both would face sharp increases in school tax rates to maintain their existing levels of expenditure.

This shows that reform of education finance is not as simple a matter as might at first appear. Those who set out to advocate more equitable schemes to pay for our schools did not intend to hurt the poor people of New York or San Francisco either by cutting back their school programs or by raising their tax rates. So proposals for DPE are often combined with proposals for increased compensatory education grants and circuit-breaker property tax relief (as discussed in the last section).

Let us now turn to the other major reform proposal: full state funding. The idea is simplicity itself—the state government becomes solely responsible for raising and distributing school money. Ideally, the state might replace the money presently raised by school districts by increasing its individual income tax rates. Perhaps the federal government might offer incentive grants to states to help them take up the full burden of school costs. The more likely prospect is that the state would assume control of local school property taxation and would initiate a statewide school property tax at a uniform rate over all local taxing jurisdictions.

Admittedly, full state funding carries with it special problems of transition. Expenditures in school districts may have extreme ranges. It is not readily conceivable that the state government would order high-spending districts to make actual reductions in their outlays, because many of the outlays of school districts are tied up in long-term contracts, e.g., salary contracts with teachers. Outright reductions, moreover, open the state government to the charge that it is destroying "quality" in education.

It is equally unlikely, however, that the state government would raise expenditures in all districts immediately to that of the highest, because the bill would be enormous and legitimate questions could be raised as to whether low-spending districts could wisely absorb a doubling or tripling of their school budgets overnight.

A possible course of action is for the state to raise all low-spending districts immediately up to a reasonable level, call it a "statewide expenditure level," require high-spending districts to curtail their advances, and, by gradually raising the "statewide expenditure level" over time, eventually close the gap between basic expenditure amounts per student in all districts of the state.

For example, the Fleischmann Commission recommended that low-spending districts be brought up to the level of the sixty-fifth percentile district, as measured by basic expenditures per student, which is to say a point somewhat above the existing statewide average level. This figure, excluding categorical aids, was $1,143 per student in 1970-71. Higher spending districts were to be "frozen" at their 1971 levels of expenditure per student until the state-wide level of spending, forced upward by inflationary pressures and raised upward to improve quality, reached their level. Then a given district would advance in step with the majority of districts in the state.[16]

If the higher spending districts are absolutely frozen at their existing rates of expenditures, then, through erosion of the real value of their school dollars through inflation, they will probably suffer a gradual loss of program quality. However, the period required for the state to establish a uniform system of finance should be relatively short. If the high-spending districts are allowed to move upward in accordance with an education price index, the period during which they will enjoy an absolute financial advantage over the majority of the state's districts will be prolonged, *unless* the state is willing to pump a lot of revenue into rapidly raising the basic education support level. Thus, it is plain that obtaining equity under the full state funding model is much more difficult when our economy is afflicted with a high rate of inflation.

Full state funding does not imply that equal dollars will be spent on each student. As Stephen Michelson has said, "Equality is a ridiculous place to end school finance, but it is a good place to start."[17] There are two main bases for spending different sums on different students: prices of inputs and characteristics of students. As the Fleischmann Commission stated,

> Equal sums of money shall be made available for each student, *unless a valid educational reason can be found for spending* some different amount . . . full state funding must remove disparities in educational spending that are unrelated to the educational requirements of students or to geographic differences in prices of educational services.[18]

We have seen in Chapter III that means of measuring differences in input prices from one district to the next are not highly developed. Likewise, means of relating stu-

dent characteristics to their needs for educational resources are imperfectly known. Questions of values are
also involved. Most high schools offer instruction in
French. Should they also offer Sanskrit? Probably not, but
what about Russian and Chinese?

This is not to say that we know nothing at all about
allocating resources. We know something of the cost of
programs for handicapped children, of the cost of bilingual-bicultural programs, of compensatory education, of
early education, of vocational education. If big cities must
undergo special costs associated with vandalism, violence,
or even nonviolent disruption of classrooms of an order
that impedes the learning of serious students, these facts
can be demonstrated and quantified. Indeed, probably one
of the reasons we do not know more about how to allocate resources scientifically in our most costly civilian
public activity is that we have, up to now, assumed that
the localities could make all these decisions on the basis
of common sense and rule of thumb.

What can one say about the choice between district
power equalizing and full state funding as reform measures? Basically, it all seems to boil down to whether
policy in education should substantially distribute power
to parents, in particular, and to adults who live in a
given school district, in general, or whether that policy
should focus directly on the interests of children, under
the concept that a just state will deal more fairly with *all*
children who live in it than competing local districts are
able to do. Two recent quotations may help to clarify this
point.

A very important difference between full state funding
and district power equalizing plans is that DPE allows,
indeed encourages, the perpetuation of differences in educational provision. Such differences often have little rational connection to the needs or desires of school children, who are, after all, the primary (though non-voting)
clients of an educational system. DPE offers no more protection to children from apathetic or selfish adults than
our present system does. It *may* break the connection be-

tween quality of education and size of local tax base . . . in the sense that high- and low-spending districts can no longer be identified by their taxable wealth. But at the same time, DPE allows districts to trade local tax relief (a benefit to resident adults) for financial starvation of the local schools. Thus if children are protected from the uneven distribution of locally-taxable wealth, they are nevertheless vulnerable to possibly harmful influence of adult tastes for educational services.[19]

Fundamentally, what divides supporters of district power equalizing . . . from those who favor full state funding, the two "reforms" with the most current support, is the question of district choice—whether deliberate funding inequality, which is what ensues from district choice, more nearly approaches a "just" system than does some imposed "equality." This debate, in turn, revolves around the extent to which the desires of parents are to be considered in discussing what is justice among children. Most of what passes as debate about finance is really debate about the relationship between children and their parents on the one hand and children and the state on the other. . . . Justice in the allocation of school resources to children is most likely to be achieved if the distribution question is separated from questions pertaining to revenue (in the local district), then eliminating the potential for decisions based on the desires of adult taxpayers. Accordingly, the needs of children themselves will probably be more determinative when finance decisions are made by a unit of government that is less responsive to direct parental pressure than is the school district.[20]

To sum up the arguments made in comparing the two reform plans, full state funding is the plan more likely to protect children from *relative* educational deprivation, caused by adults seeking to trade tax relief for educational quality. District power equalizing leaves a market structure in place, though it reduces the fiscal advantage of wealthy districts. Thus, DPE allows the force of inter-district emulation to continue to function and probably assures a larger total flow of funds to the education services. DPE should appeal to persons who are especially concerned with the aggregate of state-local spending on education and who are not especially concerned about the distribution of education resources among different child clients. That is the bright side of DPE. The dark side is that the plan may also appeal to parents who seek to pass on their inherited or acquired status to their own children by clustering in communities that are willing to accept high school tax rates if at the same time those communities can avoid being taxed for the high police, fire, health, and welfare programs that central cities have to meet. In other words, DPE preserves a lot of the *status quo,* with possibly some higher (but bearable) local school tax rates thrown in.

Problems of Transition
In changing from the existing patterns of education finance to district power equalizing or full state funding, certain problems of transition must be faced. These have been written about extensively elsewhere, and I shall describe some of the more important ones only in very brief form.[21]

Poor Families in Property-Rich School Districts
We have already seen that finance reform, especially in its Draconian versions, could place hardships on poor families who live in wealthy large cities. Partly, this problem is an artifact of the way we measure wealth in distributing school aid, since the most common means use taxable property divided by average daily public school attendance. Certain big cities have many children who attend private schools, chiefly parochial, and many large cities have high rates of truancy. Residents of big cities have to pay for the education of their children whether they attend public school or private, and teachers must be hired on the assumption that children who are enrolled in public schools are going to show up in class. Therefore, a truer measure of big city wealth is taxable value divided by school age youth.

Next, cities often face high necessary costs of education, for they attract families with children who have physical or mental handicaps and children who are in need of bilingual programs. Lastly, cities ordinarily are faced with unusually large expenditures per capita for such services as police, fire, and public health. All these kinds of cost differentials, however, can be recognized, even if not perfectly in a properly designed set of intergovernmental fiscal devices.[22]

Keeping the Rich in the Public School System

One of the strengths of the public school system in America is that it continues to hold the allegiance of many families who are quite able to afford private, secular institutions. It is not necessary to claim that millionaires' children sit side by side in the classroom with children of the long-term unemployed (which admittedly doesn't happen very often) to see some advantages in keeping the rich within the public education sector. We do not yet have a "two-tier" education system, under which practically all the rich attend a special type of privately administered school and practically everybody else goes to institutions of the public sector. In my opinion, a "two-tier" system such as was formerly characteristic of England (and still is to a degree) represents a more extreme kind of social stratification than we have yet had to endure.

Education finance reform *might* encourage the establishment of a two-tier system. Under DPE, for example, householders in some upper-class communities might face such steep rises in school property tax rates that they would find no financial advantage in staying in the public sector. In effect, they might "buy out" their local schools and run them privately, thus avoiding a certain amount of state regulation. They might even be able to establish "company unions" instead of having to deal with nationally organized teachers.

Budget Reshuffles

Local government machinery has a certain amount of overlap between activities carried on in different departments. Cities, counties, and school districts may all run library programs, health programs, and recreational programs, to name a few examples.

Under full state funding, a city might find it fiscally advantageous to shift some of its library programs from its own administration into the administration of the school district (or districts) within its borders, for then it could more completely share the costs of libraries with all the tax-paying citizens of the state. And likewise for other overlapping programs.

With respect to DPE, the situation is a bit more complicated. In rich suburban areas, the pressure would be on the side of transferring programs *from* school districts to municipal authorities. In poor areas, the tendency would be to transfer programs *into* school districts, because school districts would be highly subsidized by the state (and most municipalities are not).

State governments could try to minimize such budget shuffles by adopting stricter accounting procedures, but there is probably no way to get around the problem altogether.

Reform So Far

All told, eleven states have taken substantial measures to improve their education finance systems in the wake of the first *Serrano* decision.[23] Florida has, in effect, adopted a full state funding system. Montana and Utah have moved strongly in the full state funding direction, but allow districts to add on power equalized supplements. California and North Dakota have considerably expanded the amounts of state aid distributed under foundation programs. Colorado, Kansas, Maine, Michigan, and Wisconsin have chosen the DPE route. (As we noted earlier, Maine and Wisconsin include recapture provisions.) Illinois has expanded its foundation program and added a DPE option. A number of other states have new education finance plans under consideration at present.[24]

The Road Not Taken: District Consolidation

A major number of our most populous and richest

states have an uncommonly large number of school districts. California, Illinois, and Texas each had over 1,000 in 1972. New York had over 700, while Michigan, Ohio, and New Jersey had about 600 each. On the other hand, Maryland has 24 and Florida, 67. Overall, in the United States in 1972, 5,114 school districts enrolled fewer than 300 students.[25]

District consolidation *could have been* the third major route to school finance reform in states that had large numbers of school districts. That is, by combining sets of rich districts with sets of poor districts, differences in taxable values per student could be reduced to the point of insignificance. The problem that DPE attacks with state grants could have been attacked directly by removing the glaring disparities in taxable values themselves.

Actually, this approach, the "road not taken," offers two advantages over either DPE or full state funding.

First, consolidation helps overcome the problem that many districts are too small to offer their students good education at a price taxpayers can afford. For example, a district that enrolls 150 high school students cannot offer a full program of sciences, specialized mathematics, foreign language, and cultural subjects except at a cost in the range of $4,000 to $6,000 a student. Suppose a state chooses DPE as its reform measure. The district, if it is to take good care of its students, would probably be faced with a local tax rate at a level unacceptable to a majority of taxpayers. On the other hand, suppose the state chose full state funding. At present levels of average cost, the basic grants by the state to the district almost certainly would be no more than half of what would be needed for a good program in such a small district. The necessary result is that the students in the given district would be offered a very narrow set of courses at the high school level. The consolidation approach would overcome this problem, except in states where populations are spread very thinly. As we have noted, a number of states that appear to have an excessive number of school districts are densely populated.

A second advantage of consolidation is that it helps to open the suburbs to low-income households. We noted above that it is to the fiscal advantage of middle- and upper-income suburbs to exclude families that have large numbers of children, that have children who require unusually expensive education programs, and that might find cheap quarters in which to live, thus bringing down average taxable value per household. Both DPE and full state funding protect districts from the extra fiscal costs of families of the first and third type, but unless the state adopts a set of cleverly devised categorical aids to meet the extraordinary costs associated with learning handicaps, neither of the two popular reform measures protect suburbs against fiscal pressures associated with the second type of family. Naturally, then, we can expect that efforts to exclude poor families (who are thought to produce an undue proportion of hard-to-educate youth) from the suburbs will be maintained even after DPE or full state funding has been set in place. District consolidation, on the other hand, would allow costs of the various special education programs to be spread thinly over large populations. Suburban neighborhoods could no longer claim financial justification for shutting out poorer families.

CHAPTER V

Education and Inflation

It is clear from what has been said so far in this volume that additional taxes for education will be sought simply to overcome historical inequities in provision of school services. This is an urgent task of the coming decade. But historically Americans have been concerned about improving the quality of education. Can we obtain sufficient resources both to "level up" disparities in provision *and* improve quality overall at the same time? In my opinion, the answer turns on whether government, business, and labor are successful in controlling inflation.

As this is written (in early 1975), the country is afflicted simultaneously by inflation and excessive unemployment. Unemployment is likely to be the more quickly cured, for the means are known. Inflation is a worldwide problem, and recent efforts to reduce it have served mainly to reveal how intractable a problem it is turning out to be. In one of its faces, inflation is nothing more or less than worldwide redistribution of income (though some of the poor nations of the world are benefiting more immediately than others). Where such major processes are in play, it is easy to imagine that inflation defies short-run solutions.

Education has long been regarded as peculiarly vulnerable to inflationary pressures, the reason being that schools are "labor-intensive." That is, most of education is provided by teachers and not by machines. In industries where physical capital is very important, improvements in technology can offset the effects of paying higher salaries to workers. For example, take calculators. Between 1971 and 1974, the price of a standard electronic calculator fell from approximately $800 to $60. During the same period, average wages in the calculator industry went up by approximately 28 percent. So instead of wage increases being passed along to the consumer, the price of the product fell drastically. Higher labor efficiency may have been partly responsible for the happy result, but it is undeniable that the chief factor responsible for the success of the industry has been new, more efficient physical processes of production.

In education, there have been no great advances in process that economize on teacher time while holding quality of product constant, and few opportunities have been taken to substitute machines for the work of the teacher, under the assumption that machines are becoming relatively cheaper instruments of production than labor. On the other hand, no one can expect teachers willingly to forgo the kinds of wage advances that workers in more technologically progressive industries receive. The result is that education (along with other state and local services, which are also, generally speaking, labor intensive) becomes ever more costly as compared with the general run of goods and services, and inflation serves to make this more glaringly apparent. Between 1971 and the third quarter of 1974, the price index for private market consumption goods (base 1958 = 100) rose from 134.4 to 164.7, an increase of 22.5 percent. The "prices," i.e., unit costs, of state and local government services went from 168.1 to 214.1, a rise of 27.4 percent.[1] Thus, the purchasing power of the citizen's dollar is falling more rapidly in the state-local sector than it is in the private marketplace.

Making the reasonable assumption that the taxpayer is going to pay only so much for state and local services, we can see a situation developing where the states' efforts to provide reform in education finance will run headlong into conflict with the education establishment's efforts to maintain a semblance of quality improvement. As long as inflation continues at a rate of at least 5 to 6 percent a year, my guess is that the loser in that battle will be education reform. For the reformer, inflation has come at precisely the wrong time—just toward the end of a substantial public debate about the issues and means of reform, and just when some of the more progressive states are beginning to take action.

The emerging conflict between reform and quality could be assuaged if productivity in education rose. At the Conference on Inflation in Washington, September, 1974, I suggested some possibilities, admittedly long-run, for achieving such a goal. These included renewed efforts to incorporate high-grade educational technology (cable television and computer-assisted instruction) into those parts of the curriculum where appropriate use can be made of it; earlier graduation of students who demonstrate proficiency and who wish to do something other than attend high school; making more effective use of teachers' knowledge of educational processes (discussed in Chapter III); and more advanced types of specialization of labor in the production of educational services.[2]

These changes require extra effort and sacrifice on the part of teachers. It is almost impossible to imagine that teachers will embark on such schemes when the best their unions can get for them is a salary raise equal to half the rise in the Consumer Price Index, which is about the situation facing them in the 1974-75 school year.

Thus, we come back to the problem of inflation. The twin goals of reform of education finance and quality improvement are compatible as and when we can obtain advances in educational productivity. Very high rates of inflation distract us from approaching the productivity objective. The greatest contribution the federal government can make to education reform, accordingly, is to gain the strength and wisdom needed to moderate the general price advance.

FOOTNOTES

Chapter I

[1]Unless otherwise noted, all data in this chapter are drawn from the following sources: W. V. Grant and C. G. Lind, *Digest of Educational Statistics* (Washington: Government Printing Office, 1974); M. M. Frankel and J. F. Beamer, *Projections of Educational Statistics to 1982-83* (Washington: Government Printing Office, 1974); U.S. Department of Commerce, *Statistical Abstract of the United States, 1973* (Washington: Government Printing Office, 1973); M. Cobern, C. Salem, and S. Mushkin, *Indicators of Educational Outcome, Fall 1972* (Washington: Government Printing Office, 1973); and E. P. McLoone, *Profiles in School Support, 1969-70* (Washington: Government Printing Office, 1974).

[2]G. S. Becker, *Human Capital* (New York: National Bureau of Economic Research, 1964), pp. 120-21.

[3]I. Berg, *Education and Jobs: The Great Training Robbery* (Boston: Beacon Press, 1971), pp. 87-98.

[4]E. J. Mishan, *The Costs of Economic Growth* (London: Staples Press, 1967), p. 142.

[5]M. Cobern, C. Salem, and S. Mushkin, *Indicators of Educational Outcome, Fall 1972* (Washington: Government Printing Office, 1973), p. 46.

Chapter II

[1]Economic efficiency, i.e., making the goods and services most highly valued by consumers, stands in contrast to "technological efficiency," which is a matter of producing some set of goods or services of given quality at lowest feasible cost. Technological efficiency, accordingly, is a matter of avoiding waste in production processes. We shall be discussing technological efficiency in education in the following chapter.

[2]At the moment, we beg the question of who are the "patrons" of education: the society at large, the local community, parents, or children. However, economic inefficiency in education would presumably occur where any one of these parties is dissatisfied with curricular emphasis.

[3]C. M. Tiebout, "A Pure Theory of Local Expenditures," *Journal of Political Economy*, October, 1956, pp. 416-24.

[4]As we shall see in Chapter IV, full state assumption of educational costs has nevertheless been recommended by the Committee for Economic Development; the Advisory Commission on Intergovernmental Relations; James B. Conant, educational statesman; the New York State Commission on the Quality, Cost, and Financing of Elementary and Secondary Education (Fleischmann); and by Stephen Michelson, Senior Economist, Center of Community Economic Development, Cambridge, Mass.

[5]*Ibid*, p. 418.

[6]*Ibid.*, p. 419.

[7]If husband and wife disagree strongly about where to live, divorce is one solution to the problem. Our laws do not allow children to divorce their parents, so geographic entitlement is presumably more binding on children than adults.

> Whereas unsatisfactory husband-wife relationships can be dissolved by divorce, there is no comparable procedure for dissolving unsatisfactory parent-child relationship (other than the passage of time); the frequent consequence is rebellion.

N. B. Ryder, "The Family in Developing Countries," *Scientific American*, September, 1974, p. 130.

[8]C. S. Benson, "Foreword," in E. Coons and S. D. Sugarman, *Family Choice in Education: A Model State System for Vouchers* (Berkeley: Institute of Governmental Studies, University of California, 1971), p. 3. (Italics added.)

[9]Where large cities are divided up into school attendance areas, the same process works even within a single school jurisdiction. In order to have one's children attend a school of superior standard, the given family often must purchase or rent a house in one of the city's high-priced residential quarters.

[10]The process of capitalization on the tax rate side has been described as follows:

> Suppose a large factory that imposed no costs on local government suddenly moved into one of two neighboring communities that had identical housing, population, tax base, and school tax rates. The tax base in the district with the factory would increase by the assessed value of the plant, so that the tax rate needed to generate the amount of revenue per pupil that was raised previously would fall. Families living in the other community, or those considering moving to either area, would see the tax advantage and want to move to the community with the factory, as long as it did not pollute the surroundings or reduce the attractiveness of the community as a place to live. The price of houses in that area would thus increase, even though the houses were identical with those in the neighboring community. The appreciation would continue until a price level was reached at which people felt there was no advantage either to living in the community with the lower tax rate and the higher cost of housing or to the one with the higher tax rate and the lower housing cost.

Robert D. Reischauer and Robert W. Hartman, *Reforming School Finance* (Washington: The Brookings Institution, 1973), p. 33.

[11]There is one way, however, that low-income households can obtain access to high-expenditure school programs. It is by choosing to live in an industrial tax haven. Emeryville in Northern California is an example. Though its residential population is small, Emeryville has very large amounts of taxable properties in the form of factories, warehouses, and freight terminals. The combina-

tion of few people and heavy industrial activity gives the place a low tax rate and the ability to provide expensive local public services. Housing is not dear, but the houses stand in the midst of factory noise, heavy truck traffic, and grime. These latter discomforts are the price that Emeryville residents pay for their fortunate fiscal situation.

[12]C. S. Benson, P. M. Goldfinger, E. G. Hoachlander, and J. S. Pers, *Planning for Educational Reform: Financial and Social Alternatives* (New York: Dodd, Mead, and Company, 1974), p. 107.

[13]Tiebout, *op. cit.*

[14]This is the kind of reason why the Nobel laureate economist Paul Samuelson found the Tiebout model basically unacceptable. See P. Samuelson, "Aspects of Public Expenditure Theories," *Review of Economics and Statistics*, November, 1958.

[15]As Henry M. Levin has said,
> . . . if equality must be brought about through educational policy alone, then educational services must include far more than instructional services. To a certain degree, the various investment sources might represent substitutes for each other in producing capital embodiment. For example, good instructional services may be able to compensate for many of the educational inputs that the family would normally provide. Yet . . . instructional services are probably not substitutable for a protein or vitamin B deficiency, a need for eyeglasses, or a debilitating systemic infection. Accordingly, the compensatory educational budget must be allocated among a variety of investment inputs to obtain a substantial increase in productive capital embodiment. . . .

See his article, "Equal Educational Opportunity and the Distribution of Educational Expenditures," *Education and Urban Society*, February, 1973, p. 161.

[16]E. Cohn, *The Economics of Education* (Lexington, Mass.: Lexington Books, 1972), p. 264.

[17]*Ibid.*, p. 265.

[18]In the last sections of this chapter we consider what some of these means might be.

[19]M. Friedman, "The Role of Government in Education," in Robert A. Solo, ed., *Economics and the Public Interest* (New Brunswick: Rutgers University Press, 1955), pp. 127-28.

[20]*Ibid.*, p. 129.

[21]*Ibid.*, p. 130.

[22]G. W. Harobin and R. L. Smyth, "The Economics of Education: A Comment," *Scottish Journal of Political Economy*, February, 1960, pp. 69-74.

[23]Grievance procedures are coming to be of increasing importance in education. They need not be confined to resolution of problems be-

tween administrators and staff; they could also be used to resolve issues between school staffs and parents.

[24]J. E. Coons and S. D. Sugarman, *Family Choice in Education: A Model State System for Vouchers* (Berkeley: Institute of Governmental Studies, University of California, 1971).

[25]We discussed external economies in consumption, otherwise called social benefits, at some length in the previous chapter. External economies of production in education refer to the apparent fact that the educational performance of a student in a given school is a function, *inter alia*, of the characteristics of his fellow students.

[26]If a family has more than one child in school, and if these children attend schools of different expenditure levels, the tax rate charged to the family will be the average of the rates fixed for schools in the categories attended by their children. Actually, it would seem unlikely that most families would practice such invidious discrimination as to send some of their children to expensive schools and some to cheap, unless, *mirabile dictu*, it turned out that high-status education, namely, college preparatory, happened to be generally cheaper than low-status kinds—vocational, artistic, scientific, and the like.

[27]C. S. Benson, "Foreword," *op. cit.*

[28]The basic voucher ideas of the OEO experimental plan are given in Center for the Study of Public Policy, *Education Vouchers: A Report in Financing Education by Grants to Parents* (Cambridge: The Center, 1970).

[29]D. Weiler, *et al.*, *A Public School Voucher Demonstration: The First Year at Alum Rock, Summary and Conclusions* (Santa Monica: The Rand Corporation, 1974), p. 26.

[30]Sequoia Institute, *What Is a Voucher?* (San Jose, Calif.: Alum Rock Union School District, 1973); Sequoia Institute, *Educational Choices for Your Child: Voucher Program Alternatives, 1973-74* (San Jose, Calif.: Alum Rock Union School District, 1973).

[31]D. Weiler, *op. cit.*, pp. vii-viii.

[32]H. M. Levin, *Educational Vouchers and Educational Equality*, Occasional Papers in the Economics and Politics of Education 74-2, (Stanford: School of Education, Stanford University, 1974). p. 5.

[33]*Ibid.*, p. 7.

[34]*Ibid.*, p. 10.

[35]*Ibid.*, p. 13.

[36]*Ibid.*, p. 16.

[37]*Ibid.*, p. 18.

[38]Berkeley Unified School District, *Berkeley Schools, Year End Review* (Berkeley: The District, 1973).

[39]W. K. Medlin, W. M. Cave, and F. Carpenter, *Education and Development in Central Asia: A Case Study on Social Change in Uzbekistan* (Leiden: E. J. Brill, 1971), p. 196.

[40]*Ibid.*, p. 200.

Chapter III

[1]R. S. Takasaki, *Training Guide in Program Budgeting: Dimensions of Program Budgeting* (Honolulu: University of Hawaii, 1966).

[2]J. A. Kershaw and R. M. McKean, *Systems Analysis and Education* (Santa Monica: The Rand Corporation, 1959), Chapter V.

[3]K. Deitch, "Some Observations on the Allocation of Resources in Higher Education," in S. Harris, ed., *Higher Education in the United States: The Economic Problems* (Cambridge: Harvard University Press, 1960), p. 192.

[4]C. L. Schultz, *The Politics and Economics of Public Spending* (Washington: The Brookings Institution, 1968), p. 19.

[5]*Ibid.*, p. 20.

[6]*Ibid.*, p. 23.

[7]The "bible" of PPBS advocates is a volume directed primarily toward military applications: C. J. Hitch and R. N. McKean, *The Economics of Defense in the Nuclear Age* (Cambridge: Harvard University Press, 1961).

[8]Paul Feldman, "Prescription for an Effective Government: Ethics, Economics, and PPBS," in Joint Economic Committee, Congress of the United States, *The Analysis and Evaluation of Public Expenditures: The PPBS System* (Washington: Government Printing Office, 1969), Vol. 3, pp. 866-67.

[9]One reason is that the beneficiaries of two different programs may be different sets of households. Even if a first group of households receives larger net benefits under one program than a second group receives under some other program, we cannot conclude that the first program is superior to the second and that the objective of the first program thus "counts for more." It might be that the second group of households, though receiving smaller benefits, was so severely deprived that the members of that group "needed" their larger returns. Economics does very badly in trying to make judgments about the relative worth of changes in welfare of different households—in general.

[10]Testimony of William Gorham before Joint Economic Committee, U.S. Congress, *The Planning-Programming-Budgeting System: Progress and Potentials* (Washington: Government Printing Office, 1967), p. 5.

[11]C. S. Benson and H. L. Hodgkinson, *Implementing the Learning Society* (San Francisco: Jossey-Bass, Inc., 1974), p. 38.

[12]Schultze, *op. cit.*, p. 75.

[13]J. Burkhead and J. Miner, *Public Expenditure* (Chicago: Aldine-Atherton, 1971), p. 198.

[14]James W. Guthrie, *School Site Budgeting Report to Oakland Public Schools* (Oakland: Master Plan Citizens Committee, 1973).

[15]These models are more frequently employed in higher education than in the schools. For an example of a highly developed education simulation model, see R. W. Judy, "Simulation and Rational Resource Allocation in Universities," in Organization for Economic Cooperation and Development, *Efficiency in Resource Allocation in Education* (Paris: The Organization, 1969).

[16]See B. A. Weisbrod, "Preventing High School Dropouts," in Robert Dorfman, ed., *Measuring Benefits of Government Investments* (Washington: Brookings Institution, 1965), pp. 117-49.

[17]Where either costs or benefits is a cost-effectiveness model extended over time, the dollar values should be considered in present discounted value terms.

[18]H. M. Levin, "A Cost-Effectiveness Analysis of Teacher Selection," *Journal of Human Resources*, Winter, 1970, pp. 24-33.

[19]*Ibid.*, p. 30.

[20]*Ibid.*, p. 32.

[21]F. Welch, "Labor-Market Discrimination: An Interpretation of Income Differences in the Rural South," *Journal of Political Economy*, June, 1967, p. 235.

[22]F. Welch, "Black-White Differences in Returns to Schooling," *American Economic Review*, December, 1973, pp. 893-907.

[23]*Ibid.*, p. 904.

[24]C. S. Benson, *et al.*, *State and Local Fiscal Relationships in Public Education in California* (Sacramento: State Senate, 1965).

[25]J. S. Coleman, *et al.*, *Equality of Educational Opportunity* (Washington: Government Printing Office, 1966).

[26]It is now common to employ simultaneous equations and two-stage least squares in the analysis, as, for example, in H. M. Levin, "A New Model of School Effectiveness," in Bureau of Educational Personnel Development, *Do Teachers Make A Difference?* (Washington: Government Printing Office, 1972), pp. 55-75.

[27]H. A. Averch, *et al.*, *How Effective is Schooling?* (Santa Monica: Rand Corporation, 1971), p. x.

[28]G. W. Mayeske, *et al.*, *A Study of Our Nation's Schools* (Washington: Government Printing Office, 1972), p. 113.

[29]*Ibid.*

[30]One exception is a study that used longitudinal data for the Richmond, Calif., public schools. See D. R. Winkler, "The Production of

Human Capital: A Study of Minority Achievement," unpublished Ph.D. dissertation, University of California, Berkeley, 1972.

[31]For further discussion of these points, see *The Fleischmann Report on the Quality, Cost, and Financing of Elementary and Secondary Education* (New York: The Viking Press, 1973), Vol. III, pp. 187-94, 197-98.

Chapter IV

[1]The sanctity of intra-district attendance boundaries is challenged from time to time by the courts on charges that attendance boundaries create *de jure* segregation and, hence, are unconstitutional. This may explain, in part, the exodus of richer families from the central cities to the suburbs.

[2]The comparison in real life could be even more extreme, because state governments generally establish minimum grants per pupil that are received by all districts, regardless of how rich they may be. If the minimum grant is $200 per student, the richer district in our example could offer its students a $4,200 program at the same tax rate the poorer district was levying to provide $1,000.

[3]For further discussion of this process of "tax and benefit capitalization of land values," see R. D. Reischauer and R. W. Hartman, *Reforming School Finance* (Washington, D.C.: The Brookings Institution, 1973), pp. 32-34.

[4]For further development of this point, see C. S. Benson, P. M. Goldfinger, E. G. Hoachlander, and J. S. Pers, *Planning for Educational Reform: Financial and Social Alternatives* (New York: Dodd, Mead, and Company, 1974), pp. 105-08.

[5]Education Commission of the States, *Major Changes in School Finance: Statehouse Scorecard* (Denver: The Commission, 1974).

[6]C. S. Benson, *The Cheerful Prospect* (Boston: Houghton Mifflin Company, 1965), p. 14.

[7]For discussion of this argument, see E. Clark, "The Education and Training Investment Program," in S. J. Mushkin, ed., *State Aids for Human Services in a Federal System* (Washington: Public Service Laboratory, Georgetown University, 1974), pp. 190-92.

[8]C. S. Benson and H. L. Hodgkinson, *Implementing the Learning Society* (San Francisco: Jossey-Bass Publishers, 1974), Chapter 4.

[9]G. A. Hickrod, *Final Report of the Superintendent's Advisory Committee on School Finance* (Springfield, Ill.: State Education Department, 1973), p. 104.

[10]For discussion of a formula for a circuit breaker that was intended to be applicable to homeowners and renters alike, see C. S. Benson, *et al., Final Report to the Select Committee on School District Finance* (Sacramento: State Senate, 1972), Vol. I, Chapter 2.

[11]Equal treatment of equals is sometimes referred to as the "principle of horizontal equity," in contrast to the idea of "vertical equity," which deals with how government should act toward families that differ in important characteristics, such as income. As indicated above, economics has relatively little to offer in establishing criteria of vertical equity. However, economic analysis often can be used to reveal the effects of different public programs on different income groups, at least in first-approximation terms. If heavily subsidized public universities enroll few students from low-income homes, this fact might be scrutinized under the concept of vertical equity.

[12]H. C. Morrison, *School Revenue* (Chicago: University of Chicago Press, 1930).

[13]This "kinked" form of a DPE schedule was proposed by the author and his colleagues to the California Senate as a preferred response to the *Serrano* problem. See C. S. Benson, *et al., Final Report, op. cit.,* Chapter 4.

[14]On the other hand, a very large district, like, say, New York City, might be concerned about what its DPE choices would do to the state budget and, hence, the possible need for higher state taxes that would fall on New York City residents, as well, of course, as on all residents of the state.

[15]A considerable argument, unfortunately not easily resolved with available data, has gone on about which districts would respond most aggressively to state sharing offers. Because low-wealth districts have large state matching ratios, i.e., receive 90¢ of state money for each school dollar they spend, some economists hold that low-wealth districts will overspend because of the great subsidies they receive. But low-wealth districts get no break on *tax rate* over high-wealth districts. If a citizen is asked whether he will support certain improvements in his local school program that cost $200 per student, his probable question is: What does it amount to on the tax rate? The answer under DPE would be the same in rich and poor districts alike, but if certain districts are inhabited mainly by rich people, they might be more easily able to accept the tax rise to finance the educational improvements. For a discussion of this controversy, see W. N. Grubb and S. Michelson, *States and Schools* (Lexington, Mass.: Lexington Books, 1974).

[16]*The Fleischmann Report on the Quality, Cost, and Financing of Elementary and Secondary Education in New York State* (New York: The Viking Press, 1973), Vol. I, pp. 63-73.

[17]S. Michelson, "What is a 'Just' System for Financing Schools? An Evaluation of Alternative Reforms," *Law and Contemporary Problems,* Winter-Spring, 1974, Vol. 38, No. 3, p. 442.

[18]*Fleischmann Report, op. cit.,* pp. 62, 63.

[19]C. Benson, P. Goldfinger, G. Hoachlander, and J. Pers, *op. cit.,* p. 57.

[20]S. Michelson, *op. cit.,* pp. 437-57.

[21]For discussion of problems of transition, see C. S. Benson, "The Transition to a New School Finance System," in J. Pincus, ed., *School Finance in Transition: The Courts and Educational Reform* (Cambridge: Ballinger Publishing Company, 1974), pp. 151-75, and C. S. Benson, "How to Beat *Serrano*: Rules for the Rich," *Saturday Review*, December, 1972, pp. 35-37.

[22]For some suggestions, see C. S. Benson, "The Transition to a New School Finance System," *op. cit.*, pp. 165-71.

[23]W. N. Grubb, "The First Round of Legislative Reforms in the Post-*Serrano* World," *Law and Contemporary Problems*, Winter-Spring, 1974, Vol. 38, No. 3, pp. 459-92.

[24]Education Commission of the States, *op. cit.*, Appendix I, pp. 34-35.

[25]W. V. Grant, and C. G. Lind, *Digest of Educational Statistics* (Washington: Government Printing Office, 1974), p. 53.

Chapter V

[1]U.S. Department of Commerce, *Survey of Current Business*, November, 1974, Vol. 54, No. 11, p. S-2.

[2]The Health, Education, and Welfare, Income Security, Social Services Conference on Inflation, *Report* (Washington: Government Printing Office, 1974) pp. 726-33.